THE ONE I WON

The One I Won

SHIV DHAWAN

**THE ONE
I WON**

SHIV DHAWAN

THE ONE I WON

SHIV DHAWAN

ACKNOWLEDGEMENTS

"This book is dedicated to everyone who carried me through this difficult journey. First and foremost, my immediate and extended family, the "Pushpanjali Pals". My parents – Vinod & Neena Dhawan, Kammy, my sisters – Shivani, Srishti, Siya, Neha, Sheeba and Karishma. My brothers – Sahil, Uday and Satpal Bhaiya & Rajni Didi, Tai, Kakashri, Shonali Mami, Sherry Mamoo, Bua and Sudhir Uncle, Anu Aunty and Shaleen Uncle, Hitesh Uncle and Vatsala Aunty, Nana and Nani, My masis, my brother in laws - Sahil, Aman, Vaibhav and Kabir and most of all, Angela Aunty. Without your support and our unity in this battle, we just couldn't have done it. My Samridh and Samaira, you don't know how much you helped. My house staff – Om Prakash, Vishnu, Shankar, Dharamvir, Sibram & Savita, Ramadhar and the rest that worked round the clock and whose efforts remained the most underrated; their hard work was the fuel for the machine that kept me going. Qaari Sahab for his selfless prayers. Samresh for all his massages, Pappu, Bhairov and Bhawani for answering their call to service every day. Manchester United football club for obvious reasons. Ravi Uncle, Shyama Aunty and Dr. Trehan for arranging the most special service for me at Medanta. My doctors – Dr. Ashok Vaid, Dr. Devender Sharma, Dr. Kanchan Kaur, Dr. Sandeep Bali, Dr. Kirti and all the nurses at Medanta for giving me my

life back, especially Dr. Devender who continues to give me strength when I am at my weakest. Dr. Chiranjiv for clearing my doubts at all odd hours. Raju Uncle for instilling his astrological assurances. My friends who were unfamiliar with the situation that they found themselves in but tried their level best to sail through it as smoothly as possible. Everyone at IOT, VNS, Soul and the Airbnb. God or the unknown superpower we find ourselves subordinate to – you comforted me in my time of need and proved your reality over fiction."

SHIV DHAWAN

THE ONE I WON

Text Shiv Dhawan
Design Shiv Dhawan & German Creative
Copyright © Shiv Dhawan
Text is private and confidential

First print October 2020

www.lulu.com

SHIV DHAWAN

INTRODUCTION	10
Chapter 1 - **The Story of Me**	14
Chapter 2 - **Life is Peaking**	23
Chapter 3 - **The First Slip**	29
Chapter 4 - **One Hell of a Summer**	39
Chapter 5 - **Being Strong is the Only Option**	65
Chapter 6 - **The Test for Life**	82
Chapter 7 - **The Battle was Over but the War Raged on**	107
Chapter 8 - **2020 is Cancelled**	131
Chapter 9 - **The Weight is Over**	152

THE ONE I WON

...Worry about my health, I did the most
But to contribute to its wealth? I can't boast
Relying on an unconstructed white lie
To say whenever asked if I'd die:

"Anxiety about my health will one day save
This heart from being a muffled drum
beating towards the grave"

Sleepless nights that these thoughts will make
The sun will shine when the dawn does break
Upon a message that to me was unknown
To use the strength my all can make
To do it for me, my family, my friends and on my own...

August, 2019

Introduction

I'll be the first to admit that I am a hypochondriac. I've always felt anxious at the first sign of even the smallest potential symptoms of an illness and it doesn't help that my lifestyle hasn't always been the best. So, in April 2019, at the age of 26, when I started experiencing symptoms that I couldn't explain, naturally, I started to worry. After numerous visits to the family doctor and a scan, I was told it was nothing to be concerned about. My family and friends told me that I was overreacting and it was all in my head.

Four months later, I was officially diagnosed with Hodgkin's Lymphoma, a relatively aggressive, but thankfully, relatively easily treated type of cancer. This book covers my story from before my diagnosis in early 2019 to the end of my chemotherapy treatment in February 2020 and then the months following, in which the world was rapidly pulled into the grips of a global pandemic called Covid-19.

The reason for writing my story is so that I can firmly put my cancer days behind me. By pouring it all out onto these pages, I hope to avoid continually being asked the inevitable questions about my illness and treatment as I continue my life. It's only been six months since my treatment ended but I am already fed up of answering, to myself and others, the same questions about what happened, how I felt, how I feel now and so on. So I've decided to write it all down in this book, all in one place. A final and fitting end to my cancer experience.

When I arrived back to London in March 2020, after my chemotherapy had finished in India, I deleted all my Instagram posts that mentioned cancer. I wanted to forget about it and move on with my life. Writing it all down one last time and moving on feels like the only way forward. I can simply give this book to whoever is interested and allow them to read it in their own time.

While I am not embarrassed or ashamed of what I have been through, I do not want cancer to define me. I don't want to be known as a 'survivor' or 'that guy who had cancer.' It was a part of my life but it's not me. I'm wearing the same clothes that I did before my cancer diagnosis and working and chilling, just the same as before. And yet, for some reason, I feel pressure to out-do myself in order to prove to others that I am more than 'Mr Cancer'. I hope my experiences will drive me forward, but I will not let the story end there.

The doctors have reassured me that the cancer is not likely to come back, but in my head, I need some further form of closure. I want to close that chapter of my life in some way, yet not forget my experience completely and lose sight of the lessons I learnt along the way.

1

THE STORY OF ME

*"Everything I have was meant for me,
Everything I am was meant to be."*

I was born in June 1992. India had just opened up its economy after decades of sluggish economic growth under a Nehruvian socialist ideology and a new generation of optimistic enterprising baby boomers were taking the new opportunities in their stride. My father had started a business of manufacturing and exporting ready-made garments to the UK in the 80s and he was fairly well-to-do. I was the youngest in a family of 6 and the only son. It could be argued that I was sheltered by my parents, mollycoddled by carers and protected by my sisters. Growing up in 90s India was fun yet simple. We had missed the times of previous decades when the country struggled in the grips of poverty. We grew up in an India that was finding its own new culture with Western influences amalgamated with its traditional values. A booming economy created a new ruling upper middle and upper class in the country that was well exposed to Western ways of life, yet very stubborn on letting go of their conventional Indian mindsets. New industries rose up but with orthodox bureaucracy and red-tapism still cardinal to their operations. As a toddler and child, we would travel all over the world with family friends and most of our wardrobes and toys were procured on these trips. At home, TV was dominated by American shows and movies. Rock and rap music was imported to Indian shores via the internet, while Western sporting leagues were entertaining Indian audiences just as much as cricket had been doing for generations since. New restaurants and hotels were opening in a newly established and quickly flourishing hospitality industry, while fast food had made inroads within the palette of Indian teenagers. A new class of Indians found themselves at par with the rest of the world.

At school, we often found ourselves challenging authority and the rules in a quest to remove the shackles that were bestowed upon us by parents and teachers. We mirrored our generation growing up in the West. Our ideas of recreation, indulgence, sex, religion were more in tandem with our first world counterparts rather than the proceeding generation of Indians or even with some of our own peers that were from more conventional backgrounds. I was a product of my circumstances just like everyone else is.

I was fortunate to be born into a business family of exporters with interest in other industries too, such as hospitality. I grew up heavily influenced by the content I consumed. I was fascinated with the music tastes and interests of my sisters. I also started watching football at the age of 9 and it soon became the essence of my life from then onwards; I always found myself either playing football or watching it. My support for Manchester United became fanatic, to the extent I even vowed to plan my career around my passion for the reds. And in a way, I realised that dream later on in life. I was fairly popular in school, I strived to be the 'cool' kid at all times. In that effort, I suppose I made many questionable choices but I guess that was the quintessential privileged teenager in South Delhi at the time. From bullying to breaking the rules, I indulged in the most mischievous opportunities. However, this was always shadowed by my academic and sporting achievements. I was always able to achieve good scores to please my mother (the single senior most authoritative figure in my life at the time) and stayed participative on the sports field just enough to remain popular amongst the girls and the hard boys of my school.

SHIV DHAWAN

I grew up with the comfort of knowing that one day I would inherit my father's financial legacy. By default. This gave me the comfort of not thinking about my own career preferences throughout my schooling life. When the time came to choose an undergraduate programme, I debated whether it was even necessary. I decided to use that opportunity to move to the UK and watch football for 3 years. An absolute dream. There were no two options in my head. It was either The University of Manchester or no university at all. Much to my delight, I managed to simmer down the distractions just in time to bag an admission there. In 2010, I headed from Delhi to Manchester. University definitely changed my life in more ways than one. I met some of the best people, had unparalleled experiences and made further questionable health decisions. I found myself deeply imbibed with English culture in early 2010's Manchester. With an allowance that was unheard of in my English friendship circles, I found myself frequenting all kinds of clubs: football clubs and night clubs. My father funded my entire university experience and left very little room for me to complain.

After finishing university, I moved back to India to receive the baton from my father and take on his business. Young, impulsive and naïve I was placed at the top of the organisation. My father and I quickly realised it may have been too early for me to make that move and I decided to have another year in England under the disguise of a Master's degree. I moved to London in 2015 to study at the London School of Economics. It was only fitting that I'd go there as all 3 of my sisters had done a stint at LSE. In my head, I had fulfilled my mother's goal of having raised 4 well-educated children. However, my father's idea of success was somewhat different. Reluctantly he agreed to let me buy some more time in the hope that I would find some sort of maturity and responsibility with age and come back home to carry on his business with a more focused approach. I didn't complain. I enjoyed that year to the fullest. Adding to my arsenal of football matches, concerts, holidays with mates, festivals, I wasn't making any efforts to repair my continuing trend of bad health choices. By then it had been five years of eating processed food, binge drinking, smoking and poor sleep cycles sprinkled with very little exercise.

After completing my Master's degree, I returned back to India in 2016. Lost and confused, I finally started to regret not having a career plan in place earlier. I was still under pressure to start handling my family business but it was not something that stirred any sort of ambition in me. "You can't fix something that's not broken," was the fundamental mantra of my father and management style when it came to his businesses, but I felt like there was very little value I could add to them. His conventional way of running the businesses was not something I got on board with. A system of organised chaos didn't sit well with me but was largely successful so I couldn't argue with it.

My father saw me struggle trying to find my calling for a few months and assured me that he would support me in anything I did. That was all I needed. Within a few weeks, I had a breakthrough, one that I feel was destined to be a part of all my life. A sports management organisation was looking for funding and a friend of mine asked if I'd like to invest in it alongside him. I took the pitch to my father and he instantly agreed. I don't know whether it was his experience as a sportsman himself, his reading about the character of the founders or just the sheer desire to give me a chance to pursue my own path that encouraged him to support me instantly. But he did.

I joined India On Track in 2017 and along with my partners we grew it to become one of India's leading sports management firms. In March 2020, we had over 100 employees across three offices in different parts of India. I had the opportunity of working with some of the biggest names in the global sports industry. Some of the projects felt like a dream come true. I had finally found a purpose in my career. An industry that I was already so passionate about and felt like I could add tremendous value to. A way to stand on my own two feet, even if it was still in my father's shoes. I believe myself to be rather unconventional, quick witted and strong headed with intense passion and ambition to succeed in anything I do. I felt like could realise my full potential at IOT. My career and life was on an upward trajectory.

2

LIFE IS PEAKING

*"Life is real! Life is earnest!
And the grave is not its goal;
Dust thou art, to dust returnest,
Was not spoken of the soul."*
- Henry Wadsworth Longfellow, A Psalm of Life

It was the peak of winter when I joined India On Track in January of 2017. The fog, which mixed with the pollution to create the characteristic "smog" of Delhi, was in its heyday. Everyone at IOT was excited for the future. Their hard work had paid off, having raised an investment to secure their future, they had signed Laliga - arguably one of the biggest names in the football industry and were moving into a new, bigger office.

As a part of the deal, a director seat was agreed for me. I was joining the organisation right at the top. But Vivek, the heart and soul of the organization, decided that it would be best for me to learn the ropes right from the start. I remember my first day at office and how everyone was a bit wary of me. I realised I'd have to win their respect as a leader and their trust as a colleague. Within the first few weeks a project came up in Singapore. I wasn't an advocate of the project as it didn't make sense to me financially, but I didn't remark as much in order to avoid becoming public enemy right from the start. I tried to revel in the experience and let the team use that as a reward for their efforts up till then, and as the months rolled on, that's exactly what I did. By the end of the year, I had settled completely and was challenging the management at every step I wasn't in agreement with.

The year sadly also saw the death of my father's elder brother and my mother's sister, who was more like one of her best friends. But for me personally, it was a good year. I was working in football which allowed me to watch plenty of football. United were starting to do well under Mourinho and I got to travel as much as I wanted. Ultimately, working in football meant I could mix work with leisure. I saw United lifting the Europa League trophy in Stockholm, celebrated my 25th birthday in Berlin with my best mates, got a taste of the good life in Miami and went to Glastonbury for the first time - all in one summer. Being single at the time, I was having my fun. I was rejoicing at my new found financial independence and can admit that I attracted enough attention whilst doing it. At the time I thought this was going to be the theme for the rest of my life. Work, travel, passions and partying and with no strings attached.

Apart from the untimely death of a close relative (a sister) in August of 2018 and the subsequent depression of my godmother Kammy, the year of 2018 was also turning out to be fantastic. I had settled in well at work, brought new business to the company on my own and created a few other income streams for myself as well. I single-handedly signed the French Open, Roland-Garros, as a client. I also signed my school, arguably one of the best and biggest brand of private schools in India to IOT's list of clients. I converted some apartments owned by my family into Airbnbs and trebled their revenues. At work, I had built up enough respect to work on my own terms and not accept every decision of the management blindly. I enjoyed my position as an internal independent auditor of the decision-making that went on at IOT. I was doing well financially and I didn't have to answer to anyone about how I spent my money for the very first time in life.

Summer of 2018 was incredible. I travelled loads with different groups of friends, partied a lot, attracted attention from women and got to explore many new places. England were doing well in the World Cup and I was following them from game to game in Russia. That summer I had also been to Paris and Ibiza in what was the hottest summer on record in Europe. I had attended my first football conference in Madrid with Vivek. These experiences gave me a broader perspective about the sports industry globally. Physically too, I was at the top of my game. I had hit the gym a lot, rather uncharacteristically, and felt satisfied with the way I was looking.

My sister, Siya, had gotten engaged that year and was to tie the knot, first in Dallas around Christmas and then with a bigger ceremonial wedding in India the following year. The family travelled to Dallas for her wedding and after that I carried on to Los Angeles to spend Christmas with some of my mates there. After spending New Year's Eve in London, it was time to head back to India to prepare for the India leg of the wedding. Our family had decided to make it a large affair, much to Siya's dismay who just wanted a small close-knit celebration! I invited all my friends from England to come and witness the exuberance of a giant Indian wedding.

March 2019 was one of the best months of my life. We had an amazing time celebrating and I remember feeling on such a euphoric high. Later that month, I won an entrepreneur of the year award and I remember thinking that day how much I loved my life and how lucky I was. Kammy was seeming much better and had come to terms with her new reality and I was making my parents proud with the work I was doing. I hosted all my friends from England and everyone, including my friends from Delhi, had the best time celebrating with us at Siya's wedding. I was doing what I loved and I loved what I was doing. My life was peaking.

But in just a few months, everything changed.

3

THE FIRST SLIP

You are what your deep, driving desire is
As your desire is, so is your will
As your will is, so is your deed
As your deed is, so is your destiny
- Brihadaranyaka IV.4.5, The Upanishads

While I was physically fit, I knew I hadn't been looking after my health as well as I could have. I was drinking and smoking all the time, so in an effort to get back on track, I took up running. But every time I finished a run I noticed that I was sweating a lot. And I mean *a lot*. I wondered if it was caused by smoking too much, or I was just more unfit than I realised. I also started noticing a pain in my back, which, bizarrely, got worse every time I drank alcohol.

While I was working in India, a few of my close mates at the time were based in England. I mentioned the sweating and back pain to them and they told me to get it checked out with a doctor. I agreed but delayed going, thinking it was probably just me exaggerating and being a hypochondriac again. But over the next few weeks my symptoms started getting worse and I developed a cough. Whenever I drank alcohol the pain in my back worsened and I also started getting a terrible pain in my shoulder. I couldn't understand what was going on. It wasn't long before I started avoiding alcohol altogether because it became too painful.

Not long afterwards, I was planning to go to England for a week and had a blood test booked, but didn't go to the appointment because, frankly, I was too scared of what the results might be. I psyched myself out. I vowed to not travel before getting a blood test, so I could enjoy my time there without the anxiety or guilt of being ill. But over the next few weeks my cough got considerably worse and I even started coughing up blood. I told my parents and they suggested I get a test but ultimately played it down.

"It's probably nothing, you've just been coughing too much, that's all," they said.

By the time I went to get a blood test and a chest x-ray on 20th of April (ironically), I had been coughing for 5 weeks solid. The doctor told me I had an infection in my blood but that it was nothing to be overly concerned about. I had that surreal feeling of being right when you don't really want to be right. I didn't know at the time but this feeling would become the theme of my life in the months that were to follow. While the news wasn't so bad, the doctor did tell me to quit smoking, which was heart-breaking. I had smoked off and on for a long time and was completely addicted. Quitting would be impossible, I thought, so at the time it was my biggest concern. How fortunate I was and how naïve as well! Completely unaware of the dangers that loomed large, I left the hospital feeling devastated. My friends and family were optimistic though and reassured me again that I had nothing to worry about - the doctor had said everything was okay - I just needed to quit smoking and look after myself a bit better. But I had a feeling that wasn't the end of it.

Everyone had forgotten that I'd also had a chest x-ray that day. A few days later I went back to the hospital to get the results. They needed to 'investigate further', they said. There was a lesion in my right lung, apparently.

I was right, again.

I had been expecting them to find something, but not that. I was shell-shocked. I needed a CT scan to further understand my diagnosis, they said. The sound of a CT scan was frightening to me at the time; I had never gotten one and didn't really recall knowing anyone who needed one. It was a Sunday, so it wasn't possible to book one in, but fortunately my dad is well-known in the local community and managed to arrange the CT scan especially for me that day, so my mum, dad and I headed to the hospital. It was the first of many hospital trips we were to take. We were worried but not concerned. I pestered them for the entire duration of the journey to the hospital.

"What do you think it is?" I asked.

"Nothing. We're sure it's nothing at all," answered my mother.

"Yeah! These hospitals just want to make money, there's nothing else to it," remarked my dad.

We reached Medanta Hospital, and at the time, we were hoping it would be the last time we would see the place. We were certainly not expecting it to become our second home over the course of the next few months.

The CT scan revealed that I had a swollen lymph node in my right lung, but it was quite small - so again, there was nothing to worry about, they told me. But I knew it wasn't good. I started getting really scared that it was tuberculosis, which would require six months of antibiotics. I wasn't ready to take on a disease at that time, but I started mentally preparing and assuming the worst anyway, despite the doctors telling me it was probably fine and unlikely to be TB. Feeling shaken, I was prescribed some antibiotics and sent home.

I'll admit that I started smoking cigarettes again because I felt I was somewhat 'off the hook' at this point. Understandably, I started feeling a bit depressed after that because my social life had suddenly been put on pause, I wasn't working, my ambition had dried out and the smoking didn't feel the same. I started to worry when, after taking the prescribed antibiotics for 7 days, I didn't feel any better. In fact my back and shoulder pain was getting worse, my cough continued and my nose had started bleeding too. I complained about my worsening symptoms to friends and family, who were insistent that I didn't need to get checked again; I'd already had the scans and was obviously just being overdramatic. But I couldn't stop myself from googling my symptoms all the time. Googling my symptoms would go on to become my worst enemy, but eventually prove to be an angel in disguise.

A few days later I flew back to India as I needed to get back to work. On the 17th May I attended a work event and felt an urgent need to take a break in the middle of it. The pain was unbearable now, but what was even worse was that I felt like I was losing my mind. Every day I seemed to develop a new symptom and everyone in my life was sick of hearing about it. I was tired, had bleeding gums, night sweats and pain in my elbow. I was like a broken record, having the same conversations with everyone, all of whom were convinced it was all in my mind and caused by anxiety. I had started to fall out with my family and friends over it too. All I could talk about was how ill I felt, and, in exhaustion and frustration I would kick off with them about the smallest things. Everything got on my nerves and I became rude to them and everyone around me. I felt completely lost and isolated. It was terrible knowing that everyone, including myself, thought I had lost my mind. One day, my dad even suggested I go have a smoke when he could see how anxious and low I was, sitting alone in my room. And my dad is not an advocate of me smoking!

You're not sick. It's all in your head.

Later on, in June, I had to attend a tennis tournament in Paris for work. Summer had arrived, so I decided to start drinking again. The night before we boarded the Eurostar, I went for a drink in Soho with a mate from Singapore. After just one sip of alcohol my arm started to hurt. I tried to ignore it but it became so unbearable that there was no option but to go home. On the way back I started shivering, sweating and panicking. I thought I was going to pass out so I called another mate and told her I urgently needed help. She came to meet me and explained that I was probably having a panic attack and to forget about it. There's nothing else to be done, she said.

In my heart, I desperately hoped it was just a panic attack. I'd sleep it off and head to Paris tomorrow, I thought. And I did. In fact, everything went well in Paris, so I lodged the memory as just another example of me losing my mind.

Well, if I'm losing my mind then I may as well just let it happen.

4

ONE HELL OF A SUMMER

*"Not enjoyment, and not sorrow,
Is our destined end or way;
But to act, that each to-morrow
Find us farther than to-day."
-- Henry Wadsworth Longfellow, A Psalm of Life*

The summer was well underway. Like always, I had taken time off work and made London my base for a few weeks. I had yet another action packed summer lined up, but I just didn't feel like myself. I'd wake up in the morning, make plans and then cancel them by the afternoon. That became a trend for the entire summer. I saw my parents every morning and complained about a new symptom and began to notice the worry in their eyes.

They weren't worried that I was physically ill, but rather that I was driving myself insane. My father was rock solid with his stance on the matter though.

"This is pure anxiety. I suffered with it all my life, your grandfather suffered with it and now unfortunately you have to suffer with it. Build yourself up, eat healthy and fight the feelings," he advised every day.

I would call my mother 2-3 times a day just to feel more secure about myself. She would instil the feeling of absolute security with me.

"Don't worry. I'm your mother, if anything at all was wrong with you, I would know. My umbilical connection with you is too strong and my gut feeling tells me you're fine," she reassured me each time.

Around this time, I turned to my sisters. Living with Srishti at the time I would consult her everyday about my health issues. She was singularly the only human being who took my complaints seriously and asked me to get it checked. Srishti has always been the flag bearer of reason in our family: a hard atheist, passionate feminist and a compassionate counsellor, she plays the role of the problem solver in times of adversity. Every time I would tell her about a new symptom or the persistence of an old one, she would google it, just like me, and try to find a feasible reason for it. As the symptoms kept adding on, so did her advice to get it inspected. One day I told her my nose had bled, but again the doctors had brushed it aside.

"What are they waiting for, your eyes to bleed now? Go and get a test," she sarcastically remarked. But after April's disaster, the last thing I wanted to do was get a test.

Shivani, my eldest sister, was starting to become a pillar of strength for me too. I had spent a lot of time with her and her kids just before coming to London. I didn't really want to meet my friends after falling ill in April as I didn't want to feel tempted to smoke. So in the evenings I would go to Shivani's, burden her with my thoughts and sometimes watch a movie with the kids to distract myself. So when she was away with her family for a holiday in Italy, I missed her presence in London.

By mid-June I was waking up with headaches that would linger throughout the day and every time I ate lunch I felt exhausted. I didn't have the energy to work out anymore; I just wanted to sleep all day and I was still waking up most mornings drenched in sweat. I'd also started looking weak, lost my appetite and dropped 8 or 9kg in a short amount of time. But again, it was all explained away by the anxiety.

I started dating again and lined up date nights on apps, but in the end, was always too tired to go. I didn't even see my mates for three or four months. My world was slowly caving in and I didn't know how to stop it.

In July, I had three holidays booked - a family trip to Portugal and trips to Ibiza and Mykonos with my mates. In Portugal, I slept almost solidly for the first three days as I was so tired. My family weren't impressed but I was so exhausted and irritable that I would throw tantrums about it, like a child. Then, about a week after we got back home I noticed a small bump on my chest that hurt when people hugged me.

This cannot be caused by anxiety. It's physical, it can't just be mental.

I also noticed that I was developing rashes on my arms too. The summer heat perhaps? But the bump, no one could dismiss. My mum told me there was no point in dwelling on it and that we'd wait until we got back to India to get it looked at. So I called my doctor in India again, and once again he told me there was nothing wrong with me. I was a sporty, relatively healthy young man - I just needed to stop smoking. This man was our family doctor and had treated me and my siblings since we were children, so I had blind faith in everything he said.

Around the same time, someone I knew in India had written a post on Instagram about how they'd noticed that their lymph nodes were enlarged behind their ear, neck and armpit. They went to hospital, had a biopsy and were told it was an allergic reaction, not cancer. It sounded similar to what I was going through, so again, I believed that it was nothing.

At this stage I was desperate to get better. I tried meditation and nearly started counselling. I cancelled my trip to Ibiza because I had stopped drinking, but decided to go to Mykonos as it was for a friend's Stag Do and I couldn't miss it. But while the others went out partying, all I wanted to do was stay in the hotel room and fall asleep watching Louis Theroux documentaries while my friends were out raving. It wasn't like me at all, so I knew something was seriously wrong.

I arrived back in India and my family and house staff told me I was looking really weak. I was just as stressed about my health as I was before leaving the country for the summer. Nothing had changed. In an attempt to brush off the anxiety, I would walk around for hours in my drive way. One day my brother Satpal stopped me and asked if I was feeling okay because I had lost a considerable amount of weight. I had been trying to eat more in an effort to try and maintain my weight, so it was quite disheartening to hear that. I went to my mother and wept.

"You're getting depressed Shiv," she worryingly pointed out. But I knew it wasn't a mental illness that was getting the best of me. I had been waking up with night sweats for more than 100 days by this point, so I decided to finally get tested once more just to clear my mind. On 20th August, four months after my previous blood test, I stopped by the hospital on my way to work to get another blood test and chest x-ray to rule out anything else. Straight away the doctors told me that the lesion had grown in my lung and I needed a CT scan immediately.

It's definitely TB. I'm going to lose weight, it'll be shambolic.

A few hours later, a test specialist saw my report and told me I'd need more than a CT scan.

They needed to rule out TB and a few other things, so the next morning I underwent a lot more tests. One of them was a biopsy to test for lymphoma. As a hypochondriac, I had always been terrified of getting cancer.

Once the procedure for my biopsy had been completed, I sat in the post operation room waiting to be discharged. Still under the effects of the anaesthesia, I was in and out of consciousness. In my drowsy state, I saw a woman dressed in a nurses attire, but she looked very familiar. It was my mother. She had managed to borrow some nurses' robes to come and see me! I held her tightly and reassured her.

"Whatever the results are, together we will fight it," I said.
But inside I felt very different.

My life is over at 27.

Three days later, the biopsy results came back. During this time all kinds of prayer rituals had started at my family home. I was a profound atheist, but naturally, was feeling very vulnerable around this period.

Perhaps God is punishing me for not believing.

I'll do whatever I can to get better, I thought. Listen to astrologers, pray, allow metaphysical rituals to be performed on me; I was open to trying it all. Three days of prayers and rituals later, the mood was quite jovial in the house. People were laughing, but my dad was staring at his phone as it vibrated. It was the phone call we were waiting for. He walked outside and told me not to follow him. I held back but the anxiety was killing me, so I walked outside behind him.

I saw a single tear slide down his cheek, and I knew.

My dad walked back inside and I begged him to tell me what they were saying.

"Listen, I'm talking to the doctors… it's bad news, it's cancer. But it's also okay news. It's curable," he uttered.

On 23rd August 2019 I was diagnosed with Hodgkin's Lymphoma. The silver lining was that it was a 'curable' cancer, not just a 'treatable' one. The doctors told me that most patients were cured. At least I'm not dying, I thought, but I was devastated nonetheless. My mum broke down in tears.

"Listen mum, if you start crying then I'm done. We need to do this together," I told her firmly. She stopped crying from then on. I hugged both my parents.

"I'm gona fight it. We're gona face it head on."

But inside I wasn't feeling so confident. I assumed I would become part of the infamous '27 club' with Kurt Cobain and Jim Morrison. And yet, I had done nothing with my life, I thought. I started to feel bad for my family too, how would they survive without me? Despite feeling like I needed to mentally prepare to die, I decided to put on a façade that I was completely fine to avoid everyone else getting more hurt. My parents are quite conservative and had raised three girls before me. I was the special one, a boy. If I died, it would be catastrophic.

In those moments I desperately tried to come to terms with what was happening. My worst nightmare had come true and not only that but I had also lost my trust in everyone. They'd all got it wrong - the doctors, my family, my friends. My protective mental barrier of trust had disintegrated in a matter of minutes. It was traumatic. I even called my family doctor to ask him how he'd got it so wrong by insisting my symptoms were nothing to worry about all these months.

"I'm praying for you," was his only reply.

Sadly, it turns out that lots of people with lymphoma get misdiagnosed since they often look normal physically, so it can be quite a leap to jump to the conclusion of a serious form of cancer. But in a strange way, I'm glad I was diagnosed in August rather than April when I went for my first scans. I would have had a heart attack if I'd have been told I had cancer then. Instead, I'd had four months to mentally prepare.

Everyone around me was shocked at how relaxed I was; I was making everyone laugh and didn't seem too phased by the disastrous news. It must have seemed strange to them because for the previous four months they'd watched me regularly freak out and become more anxious by the day. But I'd go as far to say that the day I was diagnosed with cancer was actually a happy day. I finally felt validated. I had spent four months feeling terrible and not been believed by anyone around me. In some ways, I was learning what I already knew; my body had been telling me it was very sick for months. Everyone else was proved wrong and I was proved right. It was a bittersweet pill to swallow, but from that day on I realised that I know myself better than anyone else and need to listen to my own body more. But there's no point crying over spilt milk I thought.

I chose to have my treatment in India since my dad knew people there and we lived near a reputable local hospital. Life moved quickly from that day on; I had no time to think as I underwent test after test and procedure after procedure day after day. I worried that the next six months would be like that.

I knew it would be a long and difficult journey, so I immediately told my sisters to take charge.

"I'm a hypochondriac, I will google everything and psych myself out more." I said.

They agreed they would take control of the hospital stuff and liaise with the doctors so I didn't have to think about any of that, which was a great relief. I also informed my family that I wanted them to carry on as normal and not to talk about the cancer at all while they were around me.

Having three older sisters doting on me meant that I became the teddy bear of the family. I'd been spoiled throughout my life and now I had cancer, so of course I was mollycoddled by everyone immediately. Arriving home in the evenings after my procedures, I'd be greeted with astrologers, Islamic, Christian and Hindu prayers, Reiki healing ceremonies or snake charmers in every room I walked into. I was like a cow wearing a bell, and by the end of the week I was adorned with nine different bangles and sweating in clouds of smoke in the corner of the room! My sister, Shivani, was given the title of 'Chief Prayer Officer' and while they fully trusted the doctors, my family also decided to take matters into their own hands. They knew a counsellor and religious lady in Bombay, we call her Angela aunty, and they invited her to come and see me. She could look into the future, apparently, and was always accurate with her readings, they said. The first day she visited, she performed a prayer over me. She was quite loud and graphic, touching me while shouting 'Hallelujah!' which was alarming but at this stage I was willing to try anything. However, I think my nine-year-old nephew, who witnessed it was scarred for life! From then onwards, Angela aunty played a crucial role in my recovery. By the end of the treatment I put my blind trust into her words and predictions. The personal sacrifices she made to see me recover remain unparalleled. From August onwards, she would try and stay up until I slept every night and she would tell us her favourite tales from the Christian retreats she'd been on.

"And then I told Father Martin he was being attacked by a snake!", she described hysterically.

I decided I could either be depressed for the next six months or be distracted by these weird rituals, so I went along with it all. Around this time something strange happened that also made me question my belief in spirituality and such things. My dad's friend had a phone call from his priest:

"Listen, I think your mate's son is ill because someone has performed some black magic on him."

My dad's friend called my dad and asked if his son was okay because he'd been told that a tumour had been put in his chest. Of course my dad was bewildered, how did he know? This man lived in a remote village in India and had no way of knowing who I was or what I was going through. The Muslim priest was invited to come to see us and he prayed over me for six hours. He told us that a woman was jealous of my dad and that's where the black magic had come from.

"You'll be fine, but I need to pray over you," he explained.

Before my chemotherapy started, there were lots of tests to get through at the hospital. The first one was a pulmonary function test to evaluate how well your lungs are working. It involved blowing into a pipe and blowing out for six seconds. It's a test that's difficult for non-smokers and so for smokers, like me, it would be impossible, I thought. And if you were a smoker with a tumour, you had no chance. I watched another man take the test before me. He was in his mid 30s and having a general health check-up. During the test he completely passed out. The doctors woke him up and made him take the test again. Oh my god, I thought. I asked the technician what was going on and he told me it was normal to pass out and not to worry, but informed me that people are only allowed to take the test three times.

It was my turn. The first time I failed, the second time I came close to passing out and the third time I completed the test then passed out.

"Well done!" They exclaimed, as I woke up in a daze. "You've done the test and it shows that your lungs are in perfect shape."

I was gobsmacked. How on earth?! I'm sad to say that I went home and immediately smoked a cigarette. It was like I'd been given the green light to continue. I tried to quit smoking before the start of my treatment, but I struggled. It was one of the only comforts I had left, even though I knew it was bad for me.

The next step was a PET scan which involved putting radiation into the body, prompting the cancerous areas to light up in the scan. I was told this test was going to take a maximum of one hour. I headed into a special room, they gave me a liquid to drink and then I waited on my own for three hours. It turns out they needed to wait for the liquid to be digested until I was ready to pee it out. Those three hours were among the worst of my life. I was told I couldn't have anyone else with me because I was technically 'radioactive'. I hated being left alone with my thoughts and there I was for three hours sat on a stool in an empty room. It was like mental torture. Finally, I was able to see my mum and we had a nice, though emotional chat.

"It's going to get worse from here, but try not to beat yourself up about it all. It will be okay," she told me.

In the meantime, Angela aunty had predicted the results of these tests. My rational mind was telling me it's not possible to predict the future - it's not scientific - but I still believed her and she seemed to get it bang on every time. She predicted the results would be good and they were. This meant that my markers going into chemotherapy were as good as they could be. Now, all I needed to do was get through the next six months.

When you don't have any control over your future because of something like an illness, it feels easier to believe in a higher power. You wonder how these things come about and frankly, I was prepared to believe in anything. And on a deeper level, I worried that my thoughts would be overcome by emotions during this time. I was having panic attacks in private which left me panting for breath, but I didn't show or tell anyone. I thought it was a sign of weakness and didn't want anyone to worry about me any more than they already did. So to curtail it and stop my ruminating thoughts, I asked everyone to be around me all the time.

Surround me and continue like normal with your menial conversations and gossip. Don't ever leave me on my own.

I felt so insecure and in need of their company that I requested they be there to eat breakfast, lunch and dinner with me. But there was a greater problem being solved that not many people were aware of at the time. By being surrounded with family all the time, I had eliminated all opportunities to smoke completely. This was of the utmost necessity now. Smoking would've been completely detrimental to my fight against the disease and if I was left to my own devices there would have been a very minor chance for me to quit. There were around thirty relatives and family friends at the house at any one time. I had never chilled with my relatives for any length of time so it was nice to get to know them and it became something I really valued during this period. We became a team and all started seeing the cancer as a project, an opponent to beat. We needed to be optimistic and I realised that a sense of humour, in particular, was important. I remember on one occasion, while I was waiting for one of my procedures, I kept joking with one of the female surgeons who was quite attractive. I could see my mum's expression ease immediately. She realised I couldn't be suffering that badly if I was still able to chat people up!

However, while my family were incredibly supportive, it was tough having people around me who sympathised but could not empathise with me, so I started looking for support groups online. I stumbled across a girl in Seattle who was diagnosed the same day as me. Speaking to her in those early days was helpful as we could relate to each other's stories and offer support and solace while starting our respective treatments. She told me to look out for a test called the bone marrow aspiration. I didn't tell anyone but I was dreading it. Initially, the doctors who were treating me hadn't mentioned it, but then it finally came up. Dr. Devender wanted to personally conduct it himself. Later on, he told me this was because he wanted me to have a good impression of the oncology department and be sure I was in the best hands. We went in - bish bash bosh and it was done. He joked with me throughout the test and before I knew it, it was over. My family had heard and read about how painful that test was for many and were expecting me to come out in pain but I suppose they didn't account for the expertise of the treating physician and my threshold for pain!

THE ONE I WON

By now I had mentally equipped myself to start my battle against the disease. In my head, the next 6 months had to be lived through and the rest was up to the medicine and God. The prayers had started to comfort me and I was finding peace in whiling away my time with them. I suppose that one finds security from unknown forces when the known ones don't seem that secure. My treating doctor and I had built a relationship by now. A leading break through chemotherapy medicine had been suggested and procured that would certainly boost the odds in our favour. All the doctors, priests and counsellors were on the same page. The universal belief was that the journey would be tough but the result would be a victory. I would be okay one day and that was enough for me to keep going and begin my treatment. I had the best of everything in my arsenal and I was ready to take it on.

But looking back now, nothing could truly prepare me for the what was to come.

5

BEING STRONG IS THE ONLY OPTION

"You never know how strong you are until being strong is the only choice you have."
-Bob Marley

A few days before my chemotherapy treatment was supposed to start I realised I had no idea what it would entail. I hadn't been to any of the doctor's meetings because I'd asked my sisters to go instead. They had figured there was no point in telling me anything at this stage, knowing it would just build up anticipation and anxiety. But the fact was, none of us really knew what chemotherapy would be like. Was it oral medication? Radiation? Surgery? As a family, we hadn't experienced anything like this before.

During this period, my cousin Neha had taken charge of organising the information to enable the family to take a more scientific approach to the whole problem. Stemming from a successful corporate career, she tried to make sure the family remained unfazed by the metaphysical solutions to what seemed to be a clear medical issue. Being the oldest in our generation in the family and arguably the most successful, she often plays the suitable role of setting the standards for the rest of us to follow. She led the doctor meetings with my sisters to ensure a proper treatment plan was crafted.

I was supposed to start chemo on the 2nd September and on the 1st of September some of my family went to a meeting with the doctors, which lasted 6 hours. When they came back they all looked defeated, but tried not to show it. I took my dad to the side and asked him what was wrong.

"What did they say?" I asked.

I think it properly hit him for the first time then. He told me I would lose every single hair on my body, dramatically drop in weight and that everything would be very different from now on. It was the last thing I wanted to hear. I didn't want to lose my hair. I didn't want to *look* like a cancer patient. I spoke to my sister who reinforced the idea that my appearance was the least of our concerns. Why care about the way you look? You need to be healthy and get better, everything else will come back with time.

Fair enough, she's right.

And yet, I looked at myself in the mirror - stared at my thick beard, eyebrows and longish hair - and for the first time I broke down. My family looked on and tried to comfort me as I howled with emotion. It was finally hitting me too. My new life was becoming a reality for the first time.

That evening my dad got quite drunk and emotional. I knew he was struggling with what was happening. I was his baby. He's quite an emotional man, but like many men from that generation, he doesn't like to show it as it's widely believed to be a sign of weakness. Added to that, he's also a hypochondriac and throughout the whole ordeal had tried to convince me that I was just being a hypochondriac like him. When I was diagnosed, he remained strong in front of me, but I always could tell he was struggling emotionally. But my mother was probably the most affected. After all, she was finding trouble not only in coping with the situation but also in trying to trust her judgement of it. She tried to distract herself by being busy with all the arrangements but I saw dwindles of fear and concern. Kammy, who had just managed to defeat the depression of her daughter's death, was devastated. She just couldn't accept that life could be so unfair to her. A God-loving woman, she started to question the very existence of God. The day I told her that I had cancer she hugged me tightly and clearly exclaimed that if something happened to me then she couldn't and wouldn't possibly survive. So on T-1 day I had put on a façade that I was raring to go and finally get rid of this monster inside me.

The next day my first round of treatment was due to start at the hospital at 9am, but by 5am, all sorts of prayers had started in the house. My uncle, Kakashree, who prides himself on being the spiritual righteous head of our family, brought in an actual cow, which they insisted I milk there and then. It wasn't ideal, but I did it anyway! I headed to the hospital with my mum, sisters, Angela aunty and a few others. We still had no idea what chemotherapy involved, but I was pleasantly surprised when I arrived at the hospital. The doctors put a PICC line into my arm that led to my chest through a soluble pipe and I was put on a drip. I slept for an hour while that was going on before asking the doctor when the chemo would start.

"You're already halfway through it," he answered.

I was amazed. I didn't feel or taste anything! Though he did say I might get a fever, but if I did it would be nothing to worry about. A few hours later I started to feel hot and sweaty. Everyone freaked out, raised the alarm and started calling doctors left, right and centre. I was somewhat of a VIP patient and so 10 doctors came running in, before realising that I was just experiencing the temporary fever I'd been warned about and insisted it was no big deal. They gave me a paracetamol and it went away. We all chilled for a bit and watched my football team United play on TV. Essentially, it developed into my family and I having a little party and making quite a lot of noise on the ward. Upon listening to some story, I shouted and moved my drip, at which point a nurse came in and told us off! Everyone was sent home, aside from my mum. But overall, it was quite an enjoyable day, which I wasn't expecting. It was nothing like what I'd seen on TV or imagined when people spoke about cancer treatment. To be honest, I thought it was a walk in the park, somewhat naively.

The doctors told me to stay overnight for the first day to monitor how my body was reacting to the chemotherapy, and I slept pretty comfortably. I was discharged the next day and when I returned home every single member of staff gave me a hug. Dad was freaking out a bit because the doctors had told me to keep away from possible infection but I told him to allow it as it was just pure emotion emanating from everyone and it would be wrong to deny it.

"It's just a moment in time, let it happen. I've got six more months to go." I reassured him.

I was feeling optimistic at this stage. It seemed to be pretty smooth sailing just getting some fluid pumped into your body every three weeks. The only thing that was bothering me was that I couldn't smoke, and I seriously craved it. I had two voices in my head; one telling me I was dumb for still wanting to smoke, and another telling me I could just cut my cigarettes down and it would still be an achievement. I decided to sleep as much as possible to curb the cravings, and for three days I slept almost constantly. Miraculously, on the fourth day, my craving had vanished. I was astonished and grateful. Srishti had once told me that I could find all the comfort I needed from prayers and predictions, but until I took those proactive steps nothing would work. Essentially she was telling me to quit that day even with the knowledge that it would've been the hardest thing for me to do. So when I went an entire week without even craving a cigarette, I was delighted. This battle against addiction was a lonely one. I had many teammates, cheerleaders and an audience in the battle against the disease but in this battle I was all alone. It was me against my mind and I knew that defeat would have catastrophic consequences. Defeat was basically not an option at all. As I had hidden my addiction from most of my family members, I couldn't involve them whilst fighting it in order to prevent revealing the extent of its existence. Fighting addiction for me was actually harder than fighting the disease. There was a medicine for the disease, I didn't have to do that much. But I had to put in a mammoth mental effort to fight the addiction and it was one of the hardest things I've done in my life.

Up to this point I had not experienced any physical signs that the chemotherapy was affecting my body, but on the fifth day I woke up and sneezed and noticed some blood from my nose again. I called my doctor and he told me to come into the emergency room straight away. No one was sure about what to expect and we rushed to the hospital. Angela aunty assured us that it was a trivial issue though. The hospital outpatients hub was normally closed on Sundays but again, because my dad knew the owner of the hospital, the junior doctor came in especially to see me, which he said he wouldn't have done for any other patient. He told me that my symptoms were to be expected and that I can't keep making a mountain out of a mole hill every time something similar happens. At this point I asked myself whether I was being too weak or mistrustful. I'd had months of people telling me I was a fool for believing I was ill and yet it was them who turned out to be the fools. I needed this to be a turning point in terms of my trust, so from then on I decided the only way to move forward without going insane was to put my blind faith and trust into the doctors who were treating me. Dr Devender and I built a special relationship from then onwards. He became not only a treating doctor but also a counsellor and a sort of a therapist for me. He took it upon himself to ease my mind whenever I psyched out. He personally took on the onus of becoming a bridge over troubled water and in my opinion that is a cancer patient's single most important need - someone to just reassure them that everything is fine.

The best part of his counselling was his approach to handling me. He knew I had a taste for a good sense of humour and he enjoyed good banter with me. Once I went to him for check-up and by then I was wearing more than 5 bangles courtesy of Shivani. One for good luck, one for good health, one for keeping the evil away etc. He looked at my arm and asked for an explanation. He heard me out and exclaimed, "Don't give so much importance to the Gods because once you're okay you will look back at this and think the Gods healed me and the doctors didn't really do anything."

On the eighth day after my treatment I couldn't eat because I was so constipated. My stomach was full of gas. For three more days I couldn't eat or go to the toilet because my insides felt so full and bloated. It was terrible, especially when I envisaged it continuing for the next six months! The following day I took a massive dump and everything was fine again. Throughout the treatment, the most amount of trouble I'd face would stem from this feeling of constipation. Primarily because there's no simple medical solution for it. Everyone reacts different to chemotherapy and my body happened to throw up digestive issues because of it. I feared that it would cause weight and energy loss each time it happened, but the doctor told me that it would come and go in each cycle and resolve on its own. This was the beginning of me realising that chemotherapy works in a cycle.

On the tenth day I woke up to a pillow full of hair. I was gutted. The most obvious and dreadful side effect of chemotherapy is the hair loss. Most cancer patients experience it and only a few don't allow it to damage their self-esteem. I, however, wasn't fortunate enough to be one of the strong ones. It's fair to say I could be described as somewhat of a narcissist, so losing my hair and facial hair was disastrous for me. Right before the start of the second chemo, the devastation began. I noticed hair on my bed, in my briefs and in the shower. To avoid the grief of watching it shred away every day, I decided to take matters into my own hands. I called a barber to the house and got rid of most of it under my own accord. I had read that taking the onus of shaving your hair by choice is an empowering experience. Empowering or not, the hair does continue to thin out and it does shatter your morale. It shattered mine at least. However, at the time, it felt like a trivial concern. Survival was of paramount importance and these by-products and sacrifices were considered minor.

"If David Beckham can rock the skinhead look, so can you!" my family encouraged me.

So we did it, though I insisted on leaving a little bit on top, so it was more of an undercut. The other option was to buy a wig and we were given a contact to get a wig made if I wanted. I have to say that wig shopping was one of the worst experiences of my life. They gave me a woman's wig off the shelf and the whole day out made me feel so uncomfortable that I decided I'd just have to stay bald and deal with it. It was the first time I'd left home in thirteen days and it had not been enjoyable, so I came home feeling quite sad. My sister told me it was fair enough to feel that way; I'd gone out with a specific task in my mind and not been able to fulfil it, which was naturally disappointing. I had previously thought I'd lose only my head hair but soon I started noticing hair in my mouth whilst chewing food. It was time for my beard to go too.

Even though I had planned to keep it a well-kept secret, rumours of my diagnosis had begun to circulate in my friendship circles in Delhi and London. Everyone wanted to wish me well but were encouraged not to by my best friends, as I had requested them to not share the information with any and every one. A friend suggested I didn't hide but pride myself over it instead. Pride was the last emotion I felt at the time but I did feel strong. I quoted on my story on Instagram that you don't know how strong you are until being strong is the only option you have. It opened the floodgate for well wishes and prayers from all my friends and followers.

When I got home from the wig shop I had a bath, the only time I was ever by myself in the house. Then I sat and cried for twenty minutes in the shower. I was angry with myself for getting cancer. On top of that, the two things in my life that I loved the most were gone. United were playing badly and I'd had to quit smoking. It was not a good time of my life. But at least the first cycle of chemotherapy was over, I told myself. I remembered what Churchill had said after defeating the Nazi's for the first time: "This is not the end, this is not even the beginning of the end but it is the end of the beginning."

I started counting down the days…
180 days to go…
179 days to go..

There was a large mountain to climb at that point, but much to mine and everyone else's relief, at least I had started the trek. The chemotherapy side effects weren't ideal, but nothing I couldn't take on. However, the worst, I soon discovered, was yet to come.

6

THE TEST FOR LIFE

"He shall call upon me, and I will answer him: I will be with him in trouble; I will deliver him, and honour him.
With long life will I satisfy him, and shew him my salvation."
- Psalm 91, The Holy Bible

Whether I liked it or not, I had up to six months of chemotherapy before life would return to 'normal'. I thought I might as well make the most of it. Two things I'd always wanted to do was to play the guitar and learn French. I hired a French tutor but alas, my motivation only lasted three days. I realised I was not in a good frame of mind to do it. Every day I woke up motivated to adopt a new hobby but the passion for it fizzled out by dusk. Then I started hinting to my family that I wanted a guitar, so my entire extended family immediately scattered around Delhi trying to find one for me, which was amusing. It was bucketing down that day, torrential tropical rainfall that is typical in the monsoon season. My uncle and sister sent drivers all over the town in the pouring rain to procure that guitar. By the evening I had it in my hands. They were obviously spoiling me because I was sick. At most I tried to play it for 20 odd minutes, realised it wasn't as easy as it looked when Jimi Hendrix and Kirk Hamlett were playing it and put it back in its cover. By the morning I was over it. It stayed in its cover in my parents' room till the end of my treatment. We also hired a full time masseuse to come twice a day to the house. A staff member of the house, Om Prakash, who had retired after Siya's wedding, came back to Delhi from Nepal at once upon the news of my diagnosis. Almost as if he took an oath to do so, he massaged me till I fell asleep each time I told him my body ached. My legs had become weak from the treatment - as the chemotherapy destroys protein in the body - causing my legs to hurt. Fortunately, Om would massage me for as long as I wished, sometimes for up to nine hours a day! I was well and truly being spoiled. We also hired a yoga teacher to come to the house and teach us all breathing exercises. Breathing, meditation and yoga are all meant to calm the mind and give the cancer patient relief from their troubles. But frankly, it didn't help me one bit. Every time I was left alone with my mind all sorts of negative thoughts would take over and add to my anxiety. I just wanted to keep my mind occupied all the time. Whether it was with sleeping or engaging in mindless chatter, it just had to be distracted with something.

A friend of mine who's mum had recently fought breast cancer suggested I tried Cannabis during my treatment. Growing up in the 21st century I was no stranger to cannabis and the whole debate about its legalisation. I had always read about its therapeutic effects but was about to witness it firsthand. I read up on its usage for cancer treatment extensively and then convinced my family to let me take it. I had heard it would help with the pains, the appetite, my mood and my sleep cycles. That sounded like the perfect remedy to all my woes. It was popularly consumed in my friend circles and easy for me to get hold of. I was sceptical about its possible reaction to my chemo though so I decided to get the green light from the oncologists before using it. I asked my doctor and he didn't really subscribe to the idea, pointing out the legality of its usage in India. But he was engaged in a conversation with another patient on one occasion and I had the opportunity to glance at his schedule. A workshop named 'Cannabis for Cancer' was in his calendar. I called him out on it immediately and told him not to prescribe it to me, but to not preach against its usage if he thought it could help me. He agreed and the rest was history. The cannabis gummies were a vital part of my treatment from then onwards. It did all the things they said it would do. The next few months suddenly didn't look as hard as before. Get high and get massages for 6 months? It certainly wasn't the world's worst idea.

When my second round of chemo started I thought I knew what to expect, but what I didn't realise is that it would get worse and worse each time, as the chemo cells build up and the body reacts more aggressively to them. This time I developed a horrendous taste in my mouth. I couldn't eat for three days because it tasted like someone had defecated in my mouth. Once the taste cleared out, I had a 4 - 5 day break in which I could eat and then the stomach went for a toss again. By now, I realised how the cycle worked. Out of the fifteen days of the treatment cycle, I would only be able to eat for four or five days, so I needed to try and eat enough during those days to make up for the other ten days. It was a tall order and so, inevitably, I started to lose weight. By the middle of October I weighed just 56 Kgs. I was down about 16 Kgs from the start of the year. I had lost all the hair on my head and shaved my beard off. I looked considerably different.

While my family surrounded me with love and support, I started to become distant from my mates and I'm not entirely sure why. My closest friends knew about the perils of my treatment, but for some reason I started to distance myself from them and everyone else. In a way I was probably jealous of them - they were getting to carry on living their fun lives as normal, while I was undergoing six months of painful treatment and putting my life on pause. Or perhaps it was because I felt they couldn't truly understand what I was going through. Either way, it bothered us all that I couldn't chill with them; they were missing me and wanted to help me fight it alongside them. I told them that if they really wanted to see me they could swing by the house, but not to expect me to do anything. I wasn't up for hosting anyone, I just wanted to relax and be left to sleep whenever I needed to sleep. Thankfully, my sisters totally got it and decided to set up a Whatsapp group with them to let them know how I was feeling from day to day.

The third round of chemo was the worst. I started a few days late just so I could have a break and eat some more before the inevitable cycle of lost appetite and constipation reared its ugly head again. Once it began, I started forcing myself to vomit because it was easier than waiting for the gas to clear naturally. But my stomach was the worst thing. When I pressed on it I could hear the gas trapped inside. I even asked my mum to punch my stomach to try and release it, but it was rock hard. My sister Shivani (also known as Chief Prayer Officer) tried all sorts to help with this situation. She gave me cloves to eat, more bangles and even made me drop bars of iron into a river. Angela aunty prayed for me, but nothing worked. Eventually Shivani, upon the suggestion of a pundit, tied a red ribbon around my stomach, which looked ridiculous. For seven or eight days I laid in bed, full of gas and having not been to the toilet for six or seven days. Inevitably, the next day it all flushed out of my system and my sister was convinced it was because of the red ribbon! But of course, it was just the cycle of the treatment taking its course. By this point I had lost 18kgs and was finally looking weak, like a cancer patient, and mentally, it was getting to me.

Diwali was round the corner and in the month preceding there were lots of parties going on in Delhi. Everyone in the city was meeting up regularly and gossiping, so people began to hear about my diagnosis and by mid-October practically everyone knew. Most people were concerned, of course, but it didn't stop the rumours from circulating and everyone seemed to add their two bits into them.

Some people thought I had died and for many I was the first person they'd known to have cancer so it was a shock for them. Others felt disappointed because I hadn't personally told them, so they assumed I didn't think of their friendship highly enough. So, while a lot of people discouraged me to do it - to avoid having more drama to deal with - I decided to clear the air and write an Instagram post for everyone to read. I preferred to confront it head on rather than deal with the rumours and negative energy. I wrote an optimistic note with a poem at the end. This was the first time I was going share a poem written by me with the world. I had always caught my mood with a rhyme here and there since childhood, but mostly kept it to myself. I was excited and nervous about the reception it would get and overwhelmed with the response. It certainly cheered me up for the day. Every day I would look for small victories like that to pull me through.

On the 26th of August 2019, I was delivered the news I had feared throughout my life. I was told I have cancer, Hodgkin's Lymphoma. Throughout my life I have been a hypochondriac. Always lived in the fear that my bad lifestyle choices will bear a heavy brunt on my health. And I considered myself extremely weak in terms of facing life's challenges although tbf prior to this I had very few to face. I would google something or the other all the time all these years and it would take me weeks to prepare for routine blood tests, check ups etc.

Since April of this year I had been feeling weird health wise and those are close to me would vouch for the fact that I wasn't there fully mentally. Throughout this period this fear of me having a serious disease had taken over my life to the point that I had reached the edge of depression. Many doctors, my family and my friends had diagnosed me with Anxiety. And I was constantly dwindling in this mental battle with myself about whether I actually had a disease or it was just anxiety that was bothering me. In August I decided to get myself checked and face whatever the problem is. I hoped it wasn't a serious illness that was bothering me and it was actually only anxiety and once I was given an all clear I could go back to enjoying my life.

So it's safe to say that this news that I had lymphoma would be quite catastrophic for me. However, once I was diagnosed, my life changed for the better. I have found the strength to face this. My family and friends formed a protective circle around me and I have never felt so secure before. This is easily the hardest thing I've ever faced in my life but it seemed scarier on the onset than it does now. God taught me a lesson and found his way to bring my faith back. A lesson I've learnt from this is that we should just face our fears in life. We probably don't know how strong we are until being strong is the only option we have. I'm doing well, I am fighting strongly and I am going to win. Leaving this note with a little rhyme I wrote in this period-

...Worry about my health, I did the most

But to contribute to its wealth? I can't boast
Relying on an unconstructed white lie
To say whenever asked if I'd die
"Anxiety about my health will one day save
This heart from being a muffled drum beating towards the grave"

Sleepless nights that these thoughts will make
The sun will shine when the dawn does break
Upon a message that to me was unknown
To use the strength my all can make
To do it for me, my family, my friends and on my own…

It nearly broke the internet. It was shared hundreds of times and as a result I received lots of messages and phone calls, on the full spectrum from supportive to scary. I had other cancer patients contacting me for advice and solidarity, but I wasn't ready to offer them any kind of therapy, if anything I needed therapy myself at that point! But overall, it was a weight lifted off my shoulders and I didn't feel like I was hiding anything from anyone anymore.

By this stage I was struggling to sleep, mainly caused by the pain in my legs and stomach, which had increased. If I was up for 16 hours in day, I needed to be massaged 16 hours a day. The massages themselves were not the normal kind though. I begged everyone to punch my legs as hard as they could. Everyone took turns to do it because it was a herculean task for just one person. Kammy, my mum and Neha were my main picks in the pecking order. This was all in addition to Om Prakash and Samresh already taking 3-4 hour shifts twice a day, so it was not sustainable. We were on the second month of treatment, the pain in my legs was increasing with each passing chemo and my family and staff were already exhausted. My family spoke to other cancer patients to see what might help and someone suggested a medicine called Ultracet, which, thankfully, turned out to be a magic bullet and got rid of the pain in my legs instantly. It would go on to become a crutch for me during the rest of the treatment.

The other thing that helped was the prayers that I was showered with each day. I'm not religious and I don't know what prayers do, but during this time they gave me positive energy and I became dependent on that energy. When Angela aunty had to go back to Bombay to see her family at one point, my mood and energy levels dropped dramatically, and they got better when she came back. So I started wondering if the prayers were really working. Maybe there is a God? Was I supposed to be scared of him? I started questioning myself and my beliefs about religion and spirituality.

By mid-October it had been over two months since my diagnosis and of the thirty family and friends that had come to my house from around the world to support me, they were all still coming 70 days later. We had all found a new routine and in some ways, it was like having a party every day. I was kept distracted and occupied by their gossip and personalities. Some, especially Annu Aunty and Hitesh Uncle, offered much needed comic relief with their over-dramatic telling of stories and others, like my niece and nephew, Samridh and Samaira became like a lifeline to me. My sister brought the kids to visit every day and unlike adults, children don't treat you like you're 'sick'. To them I was just normal Uncle Shiv, someone who was supposed to protect them and play with them. However, nine-year-old Sam couldn't understand why I was now bald and thought it was hilarious to make fun of me! No one realised how much they helped me and how eager I was to survive the cancer and live to watch them both grow up. My uncle, who lived in Chandigarh in Punjab, moved to Delhi for a while. I would go to him every morning and have a discussion about astrology and try and work out if such atrocities could be predicted and possibly avoided in the future. Since I wasn't allowed to leave the house at all during this time because I was so prone to infection, I felt trapped and restrained, so I am grateful for the varied company and support from my family and all the others during this time.

By this point my second PET scan was looming and we all knew how important it was. It would tell us whether the treatment was working or not. Everyone started getting nervous in the lead up to it and my family had been contacting every doctor, friend or acquaintance they knew around the world for advice and reassurance. They all agreed that the PET scan results would determine the next steps. I googled the consequences of different outcomes. The general consensus was that if the chemo had worked, I could be as good as cancer free already and if it hadn't worked then they would need to reconsider the entire course of the treatment. They would need to switch to another regime of chemotherapy and try and "nuke" the cancer. I had already found a lot of trouble dealing with the chemo I was having, so the whole idea of switching to a harder one was nerve-wracking. It was a scary possibility, a test for life really. The prayers intensified during this period, we had two cows now and even Qaari Sahab would drive for 6 hours every day from Allahbad to banish the 'black magic' and pray for me. On one of these days my stomach was feeling really bad, so I phoned the doctor. I was obviously doing his head in by phoning him ten times a day, but he told me not to worry and kindly agreed to do an ultrasound so I could see for myself that everything was okay. I went in for an ultrasound convinced something was wrong and that my luck was running out, despite Angela aunty telling me it was fine. The ultrasound came back positive, and there was nothing alarming in my stomach. Before every chemo, my treating doctors would physically inspect me to check for swollen lymph nodes. On the day of the ultrasound my

THE ONE I WON

doctors, just out of curiosity, did a physical inspection but I didn't know the relevance of it at the time. I was on my way out of the hospital when I just had the urge to go and thank Dr. Trehan, the owner of the hospital - who was also the personal doctor for the president and the prime minister - for all he and his hospital had done for me until then. They had treated me with so much care and I felt indebted to them. I went into his office and thanked him. He sat me down and told me how impressed he was with my character and courage and not only that but called my treating doctors to get an update on my progress. After fifteen minutes he hugged me.

"Don't take my word for it, it all depends on the scan still, but I cannot seem to see the cancer anymore."

I felt so relieved and cautiously happy but also nervous. I didn't want to jinx it - my proper PET scan was in 10 days' time. But I couldn't believe it.

The tide was finally turning in my favour. It had been a good day, especially considering it started with panic and fear that there could be something wrong in my stomach. I went home and everyone was carefully anticipating but joyful. I walked onto our lawn with my dad for a while just to fathom the information. I kept asking him if he thought I should take what the doctor said seriously.

"He's the biggest doctor in the country, he's not going to just make a loose statement like that", he said and I delightfully agreed.

The day of the PET scan was like taking an important exam and getting your results on the same day. I knew the staff at the hospital very well by now and the radiation procedure was much better than the previous time, since I only had to sit in the room for one hour by myself. During that hour I prayed and told God I would never do anything wrong again if I could just have my life back. Angela aunty prayed over the machinery and then told me:

"I've spoken to God, you're all clear, go in." She never spoke about an outcome unless she was fully confident. This made me feel very confident myself.

After the scan there was nothing left to do but go home, leave it to God and wait to hear the results the next day. If the treatment failed, I feared I would lose my faith in everything and everyone all over again. I wouldn't be able to trust the doctors, Angela aunty, God or anyone else.

I had no idea how I would sleep that night, but it turned out I didn't need to worry about that because as all thirty of us were leaving the hospital my doctor called me into his room. I couldn't understand why, I had only just done my PET scan so he was scaring me. My mum started crying and all thirty of us headed up to the Oncology floor upstairs. The doctor stared at his computer screen with a little smirk on his face. He told me the results of scans actually come through immediately but they don't normally reveal the results to the patients until the next day. He left the room to go and check on something and I became a shaking, sweaty mess. He was only gone for eight minutes but it was the longest eight minutes of my life. My dad was on the verge of tears. We all knew that the fate of my life was encased in the words this doctor was about to tell us.

The doctor returned to find thirty people praying in the room and chatting nervously. The whole Oncology floor of staff were bemused by the sight and commotion of us all, no doubt. When the doctor came back I suddenly felt need to use the loo, urgently. I remember thinking I'm going to the loo and then I'll get some information that will determine the rest of my life.

When I walked back into the room the doctor was standing there with his arms open.

"It's all gone. You're 100% clear," he told me emphatically.

Everyone cheered and clapped and started crying. Angela aunty broke down and started rolling on the floor. It was the happiest moment of my life. I burst into howling tears of joy and hugged my parents.

"I told you I would fight this and win," I said to my mum and dad.

I had won that day. My stomach was still messed up, but I didn't let that stop us from celebrating like there was no tomorrow. I called everyone I knew in tears, including my mates in England who all started screaming over the phone even though they were at work. It was like winning the Champions League Final and the World Cup all in one day. And in fact, the next day United beat Liverpool, so I was ecstatic about that too! I couldn't describe that feeling if I had to. I guess if someone could experience being born - with the ability to actually understand the experience - then that would be it.

When I arrived back home, all the house staff were standing and waiting for me in the garden. I felt like a King returning to his palace. Over the previous months the house staff had put in so much effort; cooking breakfast, lunch and dinner for thirty people, catering to different kinds of dishes, tastes and requests. It was their victory more than mine, they had kept me alive and I was so grateful.

I am cancer free. I am cancer free.

I kept repeating those words to myself for the next week. I'd climbed over the mountain and knew I was going to live. I posted again on Instagram:

> *On the 30th of October, I heard the news my ears were dying to hear- I was declared cancer free. After two months of unparalleled insecurity and uncertainty it was the most comforting thing to learn and carry on with. It has been hard dealing with the evils of chemotherapy so it was most encouraging to know that it's only going to be temporary and I will soon return to a normal life. I can't thank god and my doctors enough for this gift. My family has been unbelievably supportive of me throughout this period and it just made the hard times fly by quicker. My friends have been incorrigible in giving me support even though I made it hard for them to be there for me at this time. I still have a bit of treatment to go before I can return to a completely normal life but the worst is behind me now. Leaving this note with another note I wrote in this period-*

SHIV DHAWAN

Broken dreams and shattered glasses
This too shall pass as time passes
Hands were tied
There wasn't much I could do
I will look back at this
Smile laugh and camouflage
And say- "I won that battle too"

7

THE BATTLE WAS OVER BUT THE WAR RAGED ON

"Inside of a ring or out, ain't nothing wrong with going down. It's staying down that wrong."
- Muhammad Ali

I thought my worries were over, but in fact I needed to complete the full course of chemo treatment so doctors could be certain that no cancer cells had survived, since some can be invisible to the naked eye on scans. I had only completed one third of the course so I had four whole months remaining, and knew it was going to get worse. So it was bittersweet knowing that the worst of the treatment was still to come and that my life would continue to be disrupted for another four months. But to be two months into treatment and already be 100% clear was undoubtedly a great result.

I asked my doctor if I could go out for one celebratory meal. I hadn't been out for two months and had been big into dining out at restaurants before my treatment started. The doctor said yes so we headed to my favourite Italian restaurant located in a hotel in Delhi. All thirty of us and a mate enjoyed my very first outing in two months. As we walked in, I recognised someone I knew. I made eye contact with her but she looked right through me. I realised she didn't recognise me! That was the first time it really hit me how different I looked and how much the chemotherapy had changed my appearance. I was now unrecognisable to some of my friends.

After my positive result, Siya and Neha went back to work in Seattle and London, while Srishti remained. The sacrifices Srishti made in this period were unmatched. She worked during British working hours from India and hardly ever left the house. We watched documentaries together and she gave me company throughout. Shivani too had side-lined her work, family and social life for me completely. She would wake up and come to our house as she didn't live very far away. I was quite selfish in demanding their complete attention and time all the time. But by November there were only seven or eight people still visiting the house every day. It felt like my support network had disintegrated and yet I still had four more months of treatment left to go. While everyone carried on with their lives, I knew I had to wait until February for my nightmare to be over. My aunt, who I call Tai, however, battled on with us. She too did full eight to nine hour shifts in our house all the time. Through many personal problems of her own she rallied on with me. She would take care of her problems in the day and take care of mine in the evening. I worried for her own health. I noticed she tended to doze off in the middle of conversations and choked whilst sleeping. My cousin Sheeba, her daughter, is extraordinarily talented in cooking and would come over every day with Sahil to cook dinner for everyone. Sahil had troubles of his own- both personal and health – but still came for me. Karishma and Uday, too as well chose spending time with me over other commitments. Everyone had their roles and everyone pitched in for me. The importance I got motivated me to get through the entire journey effortlessly. The days were dragging on but at the same time I had done three months of treatment without really realising.

With the good news of me being free of the disease, everyone had cooled off and understandably needed to get back on with their own lives, but it was a lonely time for me. In northern India, November to March gets busy because the weather is good, the wedding season starts and businesses begin peaking so everyone started getting busier around me while I remained in bed, still counting down the days.

100 days to go, 99 days to go…

One highlight though was Siya returning for a while. I had grown up with Siya in my childhood as she was the closest to me in age. We went to the same school, our mother enrolled us in the same extracurricular activities and we shared many memories and inside jokes which just involved the two of us. Siya had just moved to Seattle to start a new job at Amazon, and with the news of my diagnosis, she had to take many days off right at beginning of her new job, not to mention the 18 hour journey she had to make from the west coast of America to India. So I cherished her being there with me during this time. One evening I felt quite low and just wanted to lift my mood a little. I popped a gummy and asked Siya to come for a walk with me.

I got quite high during the walk and kept chatting to her about my life leading up to the diagnosis. Having lived in America for a while by then I didn't really ever get the chance to talk to Siya about my life at university and after that. When my sisters were with me I felt a different sort of security. They are my guardian angels and also my close confidants.

December was a particularly bad month. By this point I had lost 23 kgs and was down to a shockingly low weight of 50kg. All my eyelashes, eyebrows and body hair thinned out. I wondered how much worse it could get. My doctor even started telling me off for not eating. I told him it wasn't easy and that only eating food at home was a shock to my system since I was so used to eating out before.

"What would you like to eat then?" He asked.

"I wouldn't mind some KFC…" I answered, with a smile.

Twenty minutes later the doctor returned with a bag of KFC for me, breaking all the rules of the hospital, but knowing that it would help me keep my weight up. I even got to drink Coca-Cola, which, for my family, had always been viewed as poison. My face lit up. I was delighted that the doctors were encouraging me to drink coke and drank four a day from that point onwards! The bonus was that it helped clear up my stomach problems too.

Throughout this period, minor incidents kept occurring that were becoming a characteristic feature of our daily lives. If a week went by without tragic news, we considered ourselves lucky. Fortunately, they weren't about me for once but stressed me out just as much. It was almost as if the main battle had been won but the war still raged on.

Once, while trying to take a cosy winter nap in the afternoon, I got a call from Kammy's house. She was apparently having trouble breathing. My heart collapsed. She had suffered from blood pressure issues for a while and considering our luck at the time, I feared the worst. I rushed back to her to find her gasping for air. Everyone was frantically looking for a doctor. She was passing out. I thought I was losing her and began to contemplate my own fate. The doctors arrived and checked her vitals and much to our relief her heart was fine. I breathed a sigh of relief. Though I didn't seem to find the same relief in her own expressions. It was almost as if, after everything that she had been through in the past twenty four months, she was happier with the outcome everyone was dreading. But thankfully it wasn't to be.

My father had been going every day to the temple to pray for me. He would take part in feeding poor people free meals. On one occasion, he was in the mega kitchen of the temple inspecting how the food was being prepared. The floor was wet and he slipped. He had damaged his shoulder earlier in the year and now it felt like it was completely broken. He went to the hospital to get it checked and was told he'd have to get an X-ray. Lying on the patient bed in the hospital he looked at my mum and laughed.

"I can't believe our luck, this place just keeps dragging us back in," he said.

It felt like Medanta had become our second home by then. Everyone in the hospital knew us. The emergency department, the radiology department, the ENT's, the nurses, the transport team and even the security guards. It's probably the only place in life where one dreads being popular. The X-ray revealed that he would need to have a surgery. Yet another setback. As scared as I was of medical procedures, he decided to take an alternative route and not go for surgery. It was a major blow for him as playing golf was ruled out for the foreseeable future and not undergoing surgery meant he'd have to bare the pain of a dislocated shoulder for a while.

Towards the end of December we were all just praying that the year would end without any other fiasco. It had been an annus horriblis for us and we just wanted it to end. On Christmas eve we were all sat around the fire place in my parents room at home when my mother's phone began to ring frantically. It was my cousin Karishma. My mother answered the phone and her face dropped.

"Don't be silly Karishma", she said with horror as she began to gather her belongings to leave urgently. We were all stunned and I knew this year would have one last throw of the dice at us.

"Shonali has had a heart attack!" cried my mum.

Everyone began to fear the worst. The prayers started, the astrologers were alerted and of course we rushed to the hospital yet again. She was touch and go for a solid four to five hours. Shonali mami is my mother's sister in law and I had grown incredibly close to her during my treatment. Right from the day I was diagnosed up until the day she suffered from a heart attack, she was one of the constant attendees in our house. A passionate astrologer, strongly opinionated and great patron of gossip she made for a great accomplice to have in my posse. I loved eavesdropping into the gossip sessions between her, my tai, Annu aunty and the rest of the middle aged women that came to check on me every day. So the news of her heart attack was even more catastrophic than it would've anyway have been. Fortunately, she made it. 2019 had wreaked its carnage upon us and I think by now even the year had ran out of tricks to destroy our resilience. It was finally New Year's Eve.

Whilst discussing plans for what to do on the night Hitesh Uncle jokingly said, "I will probably be looking at the fan in case it falls on me at 1 minute to twelve just to make sure this year can't get any worse before the clock strikes midnight."

All of us decided to take it easy and just bid the year farewell in peace in hopes of a better 2020. With very little idea as to what an ironic wish that would turn out to be in the future.

January brought with it the hopes a fresh start. But news had started spilling out from China about the occurrence of a deadly virus that was starting to spread quite rapidly. It didn't matter to us though, after all it was a Chinese problem. The tail end of my treatment had approached and I was just counting down the days to the end of it. By then I was fully used to the cycles of chemotherapy, the side effects and the hardships that came with them. So with the knowledge that there were three more chemo rounds to go, the month was destined to be a long one. The days were grey and gloomy as they typically are in the winter in North India. Depression would often kick in but I had the gummies to get through the worst of days. I'd just get stoned and watch documentaries all day which started to instil a sense of normality in my life again. A new normal, one that I would increasingly get used to in the days that followed. My Bua and Sudhir Uncle had arrived from Sweden by then. Bua brought along European delicacies that, for a short while, made me forget my stomach woes. My small appetite was pushed to its limits by Sudhir Uncle's delicious recipes. I had grown completely distant from my mates by then and was out of touch with most people in my life apart from my family. With the exception of Akanksha, one of my best friends. She was the only one who didn't take no for an answer. Even if I was sleeping when she would make the cross-city trek to come and see me, she would come and sit with my family. She tried to bring me back to normality in bits. She suggested going to the malls, watching movies, playing golf and seeing other friends. But I couldn't be bothered, I decided I would resume all relationships once I was done with treatment altogether.

To keep my spirits up during those months, I indulged in plenty of retail therapy, buying all kinds of stupid stuff. An electric guitar, suitcases, even a car, which my dad bought for me as a gift. When I was younger I had set my sights on getting my first car when I was 21 and my first house when I was 30. But by the age of 27 it hadn't quite worked out like that, so my dad agreed to get me the car of my dreams and I could pay him back in later life. I asked for a Range Rover and spent a few weeks making modifications on it which kept me happily distracted.

The car was my new hobby and I spent hours reading manuals and learning how to drive it in those difficult weeks.

I also developed an odd addiction to trashy British documentary series about nightmare tenants, such as *Can't Pay, We'll Take it Away!* on Channel 5. I also loved watching *Fights, Camera, Action!* Which was a show that followed street fights. My sisters were bemused by my love of working class British TV, but for some reason they made me feel better. I started to watch Indian prime time reality TV programmes too such as KBC and Indian Idol with my brother Satpal and his wife Rajni while they insisted to massage me. Samridh and Samaira would come over in the evenings and I would treat them to a new Bollywood classic every day. We became a movie watching team. I grew increasingly closer to Samridh in this period. I relished the fact that he looked up to me and tried to imitate me in many ways.

The light at the end of the tunnel finally started to appear. I started planning for my life after treatment. I booked to finally go back to London, eat some good food without the chemo taste in my mouth, watch some football and see my friends after a considerable amount of time; something I had looked forward to throughout the duration of my treatment. Srishti, my mother and I planned a trip to Rome. I could see a new place and fittingly visit the Vatican to say thank you to the God that had become my companion in this war. I wanted to a solo road trip across America later in the year and to just spend some time with myself. 2020 was going to be my year and I spent most of January and February planning it.

On the 4th of Feb, whilst taking my weight before chemo I was worried to stand on the weighing machine. You see, the preceding month had been brutal. To avoid the perils of my stomach troubles, I had purposely trained myself to not eat much and avoid hunger altogether. I saw myself deteriorate that month and dreaded the ritualistic weigh in on the day of the chemo on the 4th of February. Whilst walking towards the weighing scale in the hospital I was a nervous wreck. Sweating like a dog in a butcher's shop. For everyone around me this task was quite trivial. However, for me, it was of paramount importance to keep my weight above 50 kgs. I stood on the weighing scale and it was 49 kgs. Now 49 kgs is a weight most of my girlfriends haven't been fortunate to afford at the best of times. I had hit rock bottom in my head. I remember trying to sleep through that chemo with the knowledge that at the minimum I had lost 24 kgs within a year. There was very little hope in my head for making a comeback from this. I knew it would be hard and long. I gave myself 6 months. I promised myself that on the 4th of August of the same year I would be back at my normal weight of 72 kgs. And I remember calculating what a monumental task it would be.

So I promised myself to give it all I had from that day onwards. I even had a couple of bananas before starting my chemo that morning and ordered a South Indian breakfast during the chemo. I gave it my all. Restrained by the limits of my marginal appetite, I tried to outdo myself every meal. I spoilt myself with food I would crave, whenever I would crave it. I started eating bad food that would be plain simple calories just to gain weight. Any kind of weight. I increased my meals and doubled their quantities. I felt a difference in my energy levels and thought that I had finally stopped the nose dive of the kilos on the weighing scales. Two weeks in and it was time to measure the results of the Herculean effort that had gone in. Fully confident and marching towards the weighing scale at the hospital. It was a cardinal moment. A sort of setting of the mood of the day that signalled better things to come from then onwards. I stood on the scale... and to my horror my weight had fallen further to 48 kg! This is 48 kgs with 3 layers of clothing, shoes and an entire laptop bag. My true weight would've been less than 46 kgs on that day. I had lost. I remember thinking that the day has started off on such an unhappy tone. I conceded defeat and scrapped my target of 6 months. In my head I resigned to the fact that it would be years until I would see myself resemble any semblance of normal again. I wasn't going to give up, but I wasn't expecting much of a return from that point.

My chemotherapy was supposed to finish on the 2nd February 2020, but because of various delays it finished on the 18th February. When that date finally came, I felt a mixture of emotions. It had been a symbolic period of my life and I felt as though I'd developed a kind of Stockholm Syndrome and become used to it. What do I do now? I looked so weak and depleted still. How was I going to pick myself back up and start working again? I didn't want everyone to see me like this as I assumed they'd lose respect for me. My mind was full of thoughts and questions as I made one of my last journeys to the hospital. I reached the hospital and again it was a bittersweet reception. Everyone was obviously delighted that it was the final day of filling my body with poison but it also meant I wouldn't be a regular visitor to all those people who had grown fond of me.

The guard opened the door and saluted me with a hint of sadness this time. The transport team were eagerly waiting for us near the lifts, they wished me well as I moved up towards the 10th floor. The 10th floor, the oncology department of Medanta. The place where I'd spent the worst memories of my life. It was one of my last visits there and I was delighted about that. The full oncology team came to say their goodbyes to me. Amazingly they were so glad about having the luxury of saying bye to me with the hope of never seeing me in that setting again. I lay on that bed for the last time and waited for the bag to start pumping the poison into me one last time. As the chemo began, I collected my thoughts and prepared one final post to all my followers about the end of my treatment with a trademark poem at the end of it. I hastily asked one of the junior doctors to print "I Won" on an A4 sheet and asked Shivani to take a picture of me holding it. Simple yet effective. Along with the picture, I wrote down the most important lessons I had learnt from the last 6 months.

18.02.2020

> *Today is the day I have waited eagerly for over the past 6 months. Today I've finished all treatment and can finally resume my normal life. Although I need a break to regain my will, my strength, my resolve and my ambitions. I may be bald now but I'm also Bold. I may be physically weaker but I'm mentally*

much stronger. I may be skinny but I'm def hungry for more in life. I'm ready.

Now I'm not one to write long notes simply because my diction and vocabulary doesn't permit me to provoke a reader's thoughts with my words. However, I do enjoy catching the mood with a poetic rhyme here and there. Lessons from these 6 months were vast but here are the 7 that I hope will outlast-

To value every being and their opinions independent of class colour or caste

To probe into our fears even if we find the outcomes aghast

To always share our findings even if we aren't allowed to run them past

To be humble about our winnings and not be stubborn about how long they may last

To keep away from addictions whilst withstanding the spells they may cast

To change our understandings and not dwell on the past

THE ONE I WON

To chew everything and not eat too fast

Because in the words of great Martin Luther king-"I am free at last! Free at last! Thank god almighty, I am free at last!"

When the nurses loaded up the final bag of chemo there was a surreal feeling of victory that went around the room. Some of my friends came with me and watched as the last chemo bag was fitted. They all started chanting 'He's coming home!', which caused the doctors to run in and remind us we were on an oncology floor and couldn't cause a ruckus like that… but when they realised what was happening, they joined in! I was on the final lap of this wretched journey and it wasn't really hitting me. Twenty minutes later, it was over. The worst six months of my life was over. I thanked all the doctors and nurses, took ceremonial pictures with them and walked up with pride towards the finishing bell. On the drive back home I remember being washed up on the shores of my own reality. As I reached home my friends had planned a surprise for me. The house was decorated with pictures of me and furnished with cards and flowers from everyone. My friends and family had gathered downstairs to start the celebrations. I was reading through the cards they had brought with them and one of them particularly summed up my thoughts.

"You're done with the chemo cocktails, now let's move on to the fun ones", it fittingly read.

I hugged everyone that was there to receive me and went to my room for a minute to myself. I closed the door behind, looked in the mirror and burst out into tears. I touched my face in the mirror and congratulated myself.

"You have done well Shiv, no matter what I say or feel, I will always be very proud of you" I said to myself. I had well and truly won.

8

2020 IS CANCELLED

"If you can dream—and not make dreams your master;
If you can think—and not make thoughts your aim;
If you can meet with Triumph and Disaster
And treat those two impostors just the same;
If you can bear to hear the truth you've spoken
Twisted by knaves to make a trap for fools,
Or watch the things you gave your life to, broken,
And stoop and build 'em up with worn-out tools:

If you can make one heap of all your winnings
And risk it on one turn of pitch-and-toss,
And lose, and start again at your beginnings
And never breathe a word about your loss;
If you can force your heart and nerve and sinew
To serve your turn long after they are gone,
And so hold on when there is nothing in you
Except the Will which says to them: 'Hold on!'"
- Rudyard Kipling, If

SHIV DHAWAN

The 18th of February was a long awaited and emotional day and after my chemo ended, it was finally time to enjoy myself. It was the first time I had drunk alcohol in nine months so of course I was sceptical, perhaps my arm would still hurt again? And what's more, the chemo drugs were still inside me. But after two glasses of champagne everything was still fine. It was officially over. When I woke up the next day, I felt like a new person. I was still bald, skinny and hairless, but I wasn't waiting around in bed anymore, I had some freedom finally.

But I also realised not to count my chickens too soon. I went for lunch with my mum and ended up almost fainting in the restaurant, which felt like a slap in the face and a wakeup call that things would not get back to normal straight away. I started eating two meals a day, rather than just one and began to slowly build my strength back up. I was excited about the future and starting the next chapter of my life. I had booked lots of holidays abroad along with tickets to Glastonbury, Coachella, hospitality tickets to the Manchester derby and memberships to private members' clubs just before my treatment had ended and was excited to get to London and start to enjoy those experiences.

When I left Delhi in March, I didn't look like myself at all. I didn't make a mountain out of it but as the months went by during treatment I looked more and more like a cancer patient and it bothered me a lot. By the time I was given the all clear at the end of October, I hardly had any hair on my body. The eyebrows and eye lashes, however, soldiered on. But one chemo after another broke their resilience. By the end of treatment, I had nothing left. I looked exactly like what I had feared at the start. I had to draw eye brows on to look a little more presentable in my head. I started to wear glasses to hide the emptiness of scanty eye lashes. Added to all of that was the issue of my appetite and weight. At the airport whilst checking for my flight to London the cabin crew were shocked to see me in the state I was. This Virgin Atlantic crew knew me well as I used to travel on that route during my uni days. I realised I was quite far away from normality still and had to get used to people staring at me. I looked like someone who had just survived the holocaust. Bald, skinny and weak. In hindsight, I had overestimated everything. My confidence, my mood and my energy levels - thinking I'd be fully fit again by early March. When, of course, that did not turn out to be the case, I ended up cancelling some of my immediate plans with friends. But there was an upcoming trip I was very keen on going on. To thank them for everything, I had booked the trip for my mum and Srishti to visit the Vatican. I wanted to start living life to the fullest. So I had made a reservation at The Waldorf Astoria in Rome, arranged a private chauffeur to transfer us from the airport to the hotel and also signed up to a private tour of all the ancient cathedrals including a meet and greet with the Pope himself.

But the universe turned out to have different plans. By this time Coronavirus was creeping into Asia, not quite headline news, but on the periphery. Like many, I assumed it would just be a disease confined to Asia and could not foresee the carnage it would cause the world over the coming months.

When I flew to London, there were only 26 cases of Covid-19 in the UK, but Italy was getting bad very quickly. As fate would have it Italy would become the epicentre for the epidemic in the early parts of march. Lombardi, a region in northern Italy, famous for its Ski resorts amongst Europeans, had a major outbreak of Covid-19. We watched hospital intensive care units run out of beds and cemeteries were turning people away. It was a grim trailer to the rest of the western world of things to come. Soon the borders started closing and shortly after flights were getting cancelled, forcing us to cancel our Vatican plans, as we didn't want to end up getting stuck there. Locally, too, in England, large events and public gatherings began getting cancelled. I had to sell my ticket for the Manchester Derby I had looked forward to ever so much. 2020, as a year itself, was slowly and steadily getting cancelled. I did, however, get to host most of my friends one by one at our flat in London which was nice as they got a chance to participate in the final chapter of my cancer journey. They got to see me in my worst state and in a way that has given more character to my relationship with all of them.

Of course, things got much worse for the UK and the rest of the world in the weeks that followed. For me, having just finished chemotherapy and thus still immunocompromised, I was on the shielding list, so had to take extra precautions to avoid catching the virus. The hypochondriac in me went mad buying

PPE kit, masks, a hazmat suit and litres of hand sanitiser! Everyone made fun of me, but I had been watching documentaries about China at the time and knew it was going to get bad. Though I had no idea just how bad.

The mood in Britain was one of patriotic optimism. Our generation hadn't really been involved in global catastrophes prior to this unlike our grandparents and great grandparents. There was a sense of collective responsibility to fight this pandemic in London as soon as the numbers started going up. On social media, memes were being made everywhere about the situation that we were all in together. One by one every country in Europe realised that there were local outbreaks everywhere and that the Italians weren't alone. Everyone was being quite optimistic about the situation and so was I. Something that can clearly be seen from a note I wrote on social media:

SHIV DHAWAN

15.03.2020

Unlike most of the world, we've been in a state of "lockdown" for a lot longer now. Even though I was on my own earlier and facing bigger threats, it seemed easier because I had the comfort of knowing the world around me is still turning. The time now is utterly uncertain and no one really knows how and when this will get over and if and when we'll recover from this. But not all is grey and gloomy. During my time in social isolation there are some valuable findings that I see everyone can relate to now - family usually comes first in times of trouble, what matters most becomes clearly visible and that in the face of a threat, hate becomes a very trivial emotion.

So in this period of everyday being Sunday, I am going to try and remain positive. Try and learn a few skills I always wanted to (maybe). Try and rebuild my health and perhaps try and rewire my outlook towards life.

When all of this ends, I reckon humanity as a whole needs time to mourn the loss of our loved ones, rejoice in seeing family & friends, take back our economies, find new normals and just let the dust settle! If we learn anything from this dark time it should be that simplest of things are the most meaningful & nothing we do and no one should be taken for granted!

My heart goes out to all the frontline medical staff, essential services workers and economically weaker people for whom this will be as catastrophic as it will be for those that will be affected by the illness. Tough times don't last, tough people do, so let's keep lying on our couches, tolerating our family members, buying shit we probably don't need on amazon and watching redundant shit on Netflix whilst we wait for the sun to shine again!

My doctor suggested I stay in London as it was becoming unsafe to fly and the borders started closing down. We all thought we would just be able to fly back in a month... how wrong we were! My mum, sister and I made a plan to shield together, which I give them kudos for, because they didn't have to decide to stay and quarantine with me. My mum was a saint and would make us breakfast, iced coffees and vegetable smoothies every day, as well as lunch and dinner, to make sure I was eating healthily and building my strength back up. She cooked three different hot meals a day for us along with a vegetable smoothie that took almost an hour to make. Since childhood I've had a psychological stigma towards consuming greens. But after beating cancer it became crucial to add vegetables to my diet. I definitely couldn't do it in its solid form so my mother devised a way to make me consume it in a liquid form. She would chop carrots, broccoli, asparagus, beetroot, cucumbers, almonds, apples and oranges. All the essentials packed into one juice. It would take a strong effort and a long time to produce but it was a sacrifice she was happily willing to make. Added to all of that, I needed to find a new addiction, so caffeine replaced the nicotine and because of the lockdown, my mother had to make all of the iced coffees my body demanded. Sometimes up to 8 glasses a day. We all reaped the rewards of her efforts in lockdown. Every day I would stand on the weighing scale and notice a substantial increment from the previous day. In order to feel better about myself, I would clad myself in the thickest jacket and even carry a bag to see an encouraging number on the weighing scale. After four weeks I'd gained 10kg and was feeling much stronger. At nearly 60 years old, my mum was also doing my laundry, keeping the house clean and looking after me. She has played the biggest role of anyone in my journey to recovery so I have a lot to thank her for.

During this time, I would watch the news all day. Sky News in the morning, BBC in the afternoon, NDTV in the evening and CNN at night. The Cuomo brothers were just as popular as the lead characters of any soap at the time. Although the three of us had stopped going out completely in early March anyway, Boris put the whole nation under lockdown on the 23rd of March. We would wait for Patrick Vallance, Chris Whitty and Boris Johnson furnish us with the details and new measures every day. But like many people, I started getting depressed having to stay inside the same premises day after day. Firstly, I started to miss Kammy, my staff and all the family and friends I had gotten used to over the last six months. Secondly, it was the whole sense of being a vulnerable person as a cancer survivor. Added to that was the need to adapt from one new normal to another new normal. I wasn't even allowed to leave for a walk. I was suddenly captive in my own home which was a real blow considering I'd just come out of my own kind of quarantine during the cancer treatment. But at the same time, things were working out for me. I started gaining weight for the first time in mid-march which I was delighted about. The time in lockdown also allowed me to grow my hair and build my immunity back up, which was a blessing in disguise.

As the days went by, I started to roll with the punches. I needed to start getting fitter physically and mentally. I started looking into work again, did an online course to learn photoshop and began doing yoga online with a friend of mine from Stockholm. Weekend nights were spent doing Zoom quizzes with mates and Srishti, my mum and I had become a trio - we would give each other facials and head scrubs whilst watching The Crown. I will admit I was still being spoilt.

It felt like the world was having a collective experience for the first time. Most of the world was under lockdown restrictions and quarantine by mid-April. Most borders were closed for all but essential travel. Working from home, everyone was gripped to news channels, online shopping and TikToking.

There were days my mood would dip but I always had my cannabis edibles and the comfort of knowing that everyone I knew and loved were at least safe from the disease. I considered myself fortunate still. Many others, however, didn't have the same luxury. The pandemic was peaking. In the UK, more than a 1000 deaths were being recorded every day and the NHS had been stretched to its capacity. In line with the global trend, a clap for the carers was organized at 8pm across the UK to show our gratitude to all the frontline staff. This became a popular weekly fixture in our house, courtesy my mother's famous antics.

"Thank you NHS! Thank you NHS!" she would scream emphatically in the strongest Indian accent from our apartment window much to the delight of our neighbours and much to the dismay of Srishti and I.

On the 20th of April, a forgetful anniversary had arrived. I had completed one full year of not living my normal life of fun and work. I was quite pensive that day and again tried to capture my thoughts in a rhyme:

20.04.2020

*I'm reminiscing today, a year to the day
My life was about go astray, I'm in disarray
No shying away,
now I look in the mirror and feel ashamed
Still searching and hoping someone something somewhere will help share the blame
This year's just been a pain,
I'm going insane
Expecting to still try and be the same when everything around me has changed
So I put my hoodie up as I walk in the rain
Adding all this shit that I've gained hoping one day this effort won't go in vain
From the top of my frame till where I carry my name*

SHIV DHAWAN

It's all in my brain and I can't let it remain
Did talking about it help?
Na, so I'll just refrain
I wish it weren't this way
I wish there wasn't such a heavy price to pay
I wish I could see this wish that day
Dreaming of days that are gonna be ok
Determined to not go back to my ways, no way
Then I wish I no more wake up in the middle of the night screaming
Checking the mirror, looking at my face
Just hoping I was still dreaming
But out of the darkness comes out a light
When our plight's the hardest we put up a fight
We move the mountains we have been assigned
To show others there is way to get some respite

By May, my beard that had been growing back in bits since March, had grown back completely. If I wore a hat, I looked exactly like my former self. That gave me the confidence to start venturing out more often. I started going out for walks as the weather became better. I would first just walk around our apartment in St. John's Wood but soon I was walking 22 km a day around central London. It was surreal seeing London in lockdown. Marylebone and Mayfair were especially deserted. One day I stood outside Selfridges on Oxford Street in the middle of the road with just pigeons surrounding me. I had set into a nice daily routine. I would wake up, watch the news, check on my work, play Red Dead Redemption then go for a long walk in the evening and later come home and watch a series. I did miss everyone in India hugely, but I was starting to settle in well in London. By now we realised we would be here for a while. The pandemic was settling down in the UK and the rest of Europe but was starting to gather momentum in India. Watching American news channels was by far the most entertaining though. Everyday I'd watch Trump give the most ludicrous of suggestions in a quest to try and downplay the pandemic and as a result, the disease was becoming rampant over there. As if the bleeding economy and rampaging epidemic wasn't enough for them, three police officers killed George Floyd and stirred a massive nationwide riot. For weeks, the Black Lives Matter protests dominated the headlines and started spreading all over the world. On Srishtis birthday, I found out my uncle, Sherry Mamoo had been diagnosed with cancer and would have to go through a long treatment. Every time I had of someone's diagnosis it pinched me but this was an uncle of my own so it was too close to home. My mother now had to deal with his whole situation after just having deal with mine. "I wish you the pink of health, god bless you" he would say to me throughout my treatment and now it was time for me to ask god for help for him.

The world was in chaos and it felt like mine might be again too. In May, I started getting symptoms again. I woke up with night sweats, lost some weight, developed skin rashes and a pain in my back. Panic set in. It felt as if I was going back to square one. I had real fears of a relapse and realised what degree of post-traumatic stress disorder I was suffering from. Every little ailment was dragging me back to the big C. Doctors, astrologers and priests were consulted all over the world all over again. Fortunately, it turned out that the unusually hot English weather was making me sweat and worry more, and the rash was just a normal response after chemo, as your skin becomes more sensitive to the sun. Whereas the back pain was just a result of my new yoga practice, something my body wasn't used to after 7 months of not doing exercise during my treatment! I breathed a sigh of relief again.

I vowed to not live like I was waiting for my cancer to return. I started seeing a few mates, drinking alcohol and looking at work and my finances with more focus. My 28th birthday came along and I was back to looking like myself again, with a full beard and thick eyebrows. My friends from all over the world did a rendition of "Dude with the sign" Instagram handle with a message, memory or inside joke they had with me. Planned as a surprise, it made my birthday feel special even though I couldn't celebrate the way I would have liked to. Ideally, I would've liked to have spent it with all those who carried me through the year and also my friends who hadn't seen me enough in 2019. If it had been up to me I would've been in Ibiza on a yacht with 50 of my closest loved ones getting flabbergastingly drunk, but that's not what 2020 had in mind. Instead I got drunk with mates over a Zoom quiz, a few came over and it was the first night I truly enjoyed since my sister's wedding 16 months previously. It was perhaps the best time I could afford given the situation I was in.

The fears of relapse at the end of May were exasperating and exhausting but once I gained the conviction that I was healthy and started to see glimpses of normality again after over a year. I was cancer free and more importantly I was still me. I had to start making an effort to move on from that phase of my life. The sun was shining, the pandemic was subsiding and it was time for me to turn the page of my life.

SHIV DHAWAN

9

THE WEIGHT IS OVER

"Life is divided into three terms - that which was, which is, and which will be. Let us learn from the past to profit by the present, and from the present, to live better in the future."
- *William Wordsworth*

The days got warmer and longer. It was almost as if there was brightness creeping back into my life. The summer of 2020 was a symbolic one. It brought along many 'firsts'. The first time I got drunk. The first time I met my mates after the lockdown. The first time I went to restaurants and shops again. The first time I went on dates again. The first time I completed an entire year without smoking. The first time I got a haircut after September of 2019. The first time Neha and Aman had a child. The best first was meeting my father for the first time after looking like myself again. My Dad, Kammy, Shivani and Siya were the most affected by my ailment and when I was physically present with them, I looked startingly different from what I looked like by the middle of the summer. In the early parts of spring, my mother rallied with me in London. In a matter of 8 weeks or so, I gained over 20 kgs. I started to look better, feel better and live better - all thanks to my goddess of a mother. In the summer, the takeaways opened up again and that was it. I would eat up to 5 meals a day sometimes. I won't deny that the cannabis edibles had a great part to play in this increased appetite as well. I weighed myself on my birthday and the scale showed 73 Kgs. The weight was officially over!

So, when my father, after months of spending time in our house in Delhi alone under quarantine restrictions, booked his flight to London, my heart was filled with joy. I was the apple of his eye after all and was quite an eye sore the last time he had seen me in the flesh. He arrived early in the morning on a hot summer's day. Although I couldn't hug him when I saw him, I saw a great sense of pride and relief in his eyes. He waited eagerly for that day for 6 long months and now his wait was over too.

As quarantine restrictions were eased, the nation began to socialise again. There were queues outside every pub in the land on the date the pubs were allowed to reopen. Although the restrictions were officially eased on the 4th of July, I took a while to get comfortable with seeing my mates again. The FOMO kicked in shortly after and within weeks I was chilling with everyone as if there was no danger looming at all. First, I arranged to meet all my mates in parks, then moved on to going on dates in open spaces and before I knew it I was hitting restaurants and pubs with outdoor areas. It was finally time to take advantage of all the memberships I had bought during my treatment. Every week I would explore a new Soho House in London or go for dinner to The Arts Club.

I had always feared that being a survivor would carry a sense of stigma with it and I worried that dating would be difficult when potential partners learned about my past. That doubt got cleared once I began dating again in June, in the way that telling them about my cancer treatment did not muster much reaction from women I met up with. So I was pleasantly surprised. And it was only a matter of time before I met someone I started liking. Soon after, we began dating. At the time I didn't realise but getting into a relationship has really helped me. Especially because she was so mature and understanding about my situation and liked me for who I was with all the baggage I carried. From then onwards I gained a companion in my battles. Given that I was still vulnerable, we couldn't give fodder to our romance in a conventional manner. We had to innovate. Every weekend we would escape to the countryside and just enjoy each other's company. It has perhaps given our relationship a stronger bond than it would have if things had been normal.

During this time the urge to test my limits kicked in again. It had been easy to avoid thinking about smoking up until then. First there were 6 months of treatment in which I couldn't even begin to think about it and then there was a lockdown in which I didn't really interact with any smokers. But now I was out and about again. Each time I crossed a smoker, I envied them. I quite enjoyed smoking as I was never really much of a drinker, so it started getting difficult to resist the temptation now that I was fit and healthy. This was going to be the real test, I said to myself. I decided I was going to confess to my family members whenever I felt the urge so that they could talk me out of it. I had come so far in my battle against addiction and it would've been upsetting to turn back from there. That was coupled with the grave danger it posed to my life anyway. Often the urges were quite strong but the thought of letting my family down and watching their effort to see me recover go in vain always made me overcome the temptation. By the end of August, I had completed a full year without smoking. There was definitely no looking back from there.

Throughout my treatment, I had waited patiently (with a pun on patient) to start living a normal life again. To look healthy again, to be with both my parents, to see my friends again, to watch United play again (even if it was on TV without a crowd noise), to go out again and to find someone who liked me again. That was significantly delayed by the pandemic, but towards the end of the summer, that wait was over.

It's September 2020 now and I've completed a full year since the start of my treatment. What a year it has been. Along with me, the entire world has changed in this year. While the world is still not back to 'normal' - and there is debate about what that will ever be again - I am coming to terms with how I want my new life to be. The whole period of quarantine has helped me to reflect on my life more and what I want to do. Of course, I have my worries too. I worry that I will be viewed as a survivor and defined by the stigma of it for years to come, if not my entire life. But the main thing I have learned is to value my family more and to be grateful for what I have. Throughout my treatment journey, my mum has always told me:

"Listen, you'll be proud of it one day."

THE ONE I WON

I am proud. I am proud that cancer didn't change me in any way. And while I am proud that I beat cancer, I'm still pretty gutted, and perhaps will always be, that I got it in the first place. And fairly so. In my opinion, no one deserves to go through what I went through. However, I don't feel sorry for myself and as Dr. Devender made me promise, I won't raise the question, "Why me?" I didn't ask that when I was lucky enough to be born in the world's best family. When I was raised by staff that loved me more than they loved their own. When I was showered with anything and everything I ever demanded. When I was blessed with a personality that is liked by many. Or when, even in times of adversity, I was given the best care. I didn't question my luck then so there is no reason for me to question it now.

Now, I believe my purpose is to leave a mark on this earth and be remembered for adding value to other people's lives. I've come to realise that we humans, being a social species, have conformed to the norms of society. Until I was diagnosed I tried to live my life to serve a purpose that pleased others. I completed my education to please my mother, I gave into peer pressure to please my friends, I tried to succeed in my career to please my father and I tried to portray an image of myself to please society. In a quest to do so, just like many of us, I failed to even attempt to leave a mark on this planet. When I was diagnosed, I realised how limited our time on this planet is and how short the experience of life actually is. Billions have come and gone from this planet and only a handful have managed to make a permanent mark on human history.

So, on the first year anniversary of the day I was diagnosed with cancer and my life was changed forever, I'll end this book with a rhyme that encompasses a promise I am making to myself.

THE ONE I WON

I don't know if such challenges will ever come back
And how much more you'll have to fight in order to just live
I only know about the things you presently have,
You still have all my love to give

I wish that when you leave this earth, you leave a rich legacy behind
I want you to leave a box of values, values that were mine
That can make an impact which is long lasting, that will withstand the test of time
To help this world become a better place and perhaps make that legacy shine

This adversity was only a chapter in your life,
And not its story
You must continue to have fun and live your life to the fullest,
In all its glory

So If another challenge comes your way,
I know you will put up another fight and be brave
I don't know how and I don't know when,
But just don't lose your will and I promise,
You will win again!

SHIV DHAWAN

"So close, no matter how far
Couldn't be much more from the heart
Forever trusting who we are
And nothing else matters"
-Metallica, Nothing Else Matters

Shiv Dhawan is a 28 year old entrepreneur from New Delhi, India. After completing his Bachelors in Management from the University of Manchester and a Masters in Management of Information Systems from the London School of Economics, Shiv joined India On Track – a leading sports management agency with hopes of building the sports ecosystem in India. Born into a business family that has interests in manufacturing and export of apparels, hospitality and retail, Shiv always dreamt of building a business of his own in sports. An avid fan of football, Shiv travels up and down to follow his beloved Manchester United. In 2019, Shiv was diagnosed with Hodgkin's Lymphoma. After completing his treatment and entering into remission in 2020, Shiv spent time in London where he wrote this book. Shiv hopes to complete his MBA and get back to working with India On Track as well as handling his family business whilst following his passions and chasing his dreams.

Printed in Great Britain
by Amazon